**Reviews for *Finding Love Again***

"An inspiring, motivational, down-to-earth, refreshing, practical guide to a universal topic. I laughed, I cried, I soaked up the incredible wisdom. Reading this beautiful book was like spending the day with a best friend, just the right amount of comfort and emotion. This is not just a book about finding love again, this is a book about friendships and relationships, the core of our actual existence."
*Susie Russell, Relationship Consultant / Divorce Mentor*

"*Finding Love Again* is well-written, sensitive and very easy to read, full of stories, ideas, and advice on how to find love, and more importantly I think, how to keep love strong for the duration. Carolyn Martinez has a knack for taking sensitive, painful subjects and, through a combination of exceptionally clear writing and good journalism, making them seem both natural and surmountable. The stories are sometimes told from both partners' points of view - which also adds to the depth and sense of perspective. All of the stories are told with sympathy and a great deal of honesty. Though the majority of the book is built around stories, the case studies are bolstered by an opening interview with relationship educator Robyn Donnelly, and Martinez's own extensive research. It's quite interesting to see the connection between real-life behaviour/patterns and theory.
*Magdalena Ball, Critic, Compulsive Reader.*

"This is an inspirational book that has the power to change lives. Martinez has a witty, engaging voice."
*Leigh Hutton, Author Jump Girl & Rev Girl*

# Finding Love Again

Friendship, perspective and practical guidance for newly singles

**Carolyn Martinez**

*For Saully, Sawyer and Caterina*
*My heart, my home, my joy*
*You make me smile every day*

*For all those seeking love again, may good judgement and good times be yours. What a wonderful thought that the best days of your life may not have happened yet.*

**Between relationships? This book is for you …**

Hawkeye Publishing Pty Ltd

www.hawkeyepublishing.com.au

ACN: 101 912 056


**COVER DESIGN**
Ally Oop Designs

**PAGE DESIGN**
Adriana Avellis

**PHOTOGRAPHER**
Stewart Hazell

**BETA READERS**
Kate Bestwick, Beth Curran, Christine Hammond, Lynette Hammond, Patricia Hammond, Leigh Lalonde, Saul Martinez, Carol Mitchell, Susie Russell, Karen Traversari, Robert Watson

**MODELS**
Tadd Andersen, Ernesto Calderon, Bruce Campbell, Kerrie Coles, Bree Cunningham, Russel Davies, Clay Francisco, Angie Francisco, Kim Holloway, Marilyn Holloway, Alice Johnson, Steve Johnson, Kelly Lofberg, Kimberly O'Sullivan, Min Ostini, Libby Rodgers, Prudence Sepp, Astrid Soiland, Chris Tola, Kristen Tola, Brian Wark, Alison Wellings, Claire Williams

**ISBN:**
978-0-9871909-3-2

This book contains personal interviews. The opinions and information provided by the interviewees are not the opinions of the publisher. These interviews are anecdotal to the best of the interviewee's recollection.

Those who agreed to be interviewed for this book have shared intimately their experiences. Due to the extreme personal nature of this information, names and places have been changed to protect people's identities.

**If doing what you've always done is not giving you the results you seek, it's time to do something different.**

# Finding Yourself Single Later in Life

Before I fell in love for the first time, I was firmly of the belief that I would rather be single than in a relationship in which I was unhappy. I enjoyed being single. I was independent, had good friends and don't remember experiencing any loneliness.

It was shocking to me later, after 12 years with someone I loved, just how much I struggled with the loneliness when I did find myself single at 32 years of age. It was a different ball game out there! In my teens and early twenties, my social circle had been filled with other singles. At 32, I found that the field was scattered with a few random, emotionally-scarred, battle-weary players. The bulk of my peers were at home with their partners raising young children. Potential partners were few and far between, and there wasn't a wing-person in sight – I had no single female friends.

Emerging from a long-term relationship into a singles space is challenging for everyone, with varying degrees of difficulty depending on the reason for the relationship ending, the length and/or intensity of the previous relationship, your age, and the make-up of the support network surrounding you.

Loss can occur through death or break-up, at any age. There might be kids involved. There might be financial devastation, betrayal, anger, hurt. You might be the one who broke off the relationship, but it still hurts. Everyone has to travel through all the stages of grief in their own time.

You finally begin to emerge from the grief … and then what?

This book offers you men and women of a range of ages who have shared their stories intimately. Sometimes, your heartache might be so intense that it feels like you're the only one to hurt this much, or to have been so lonely, angry, frustrated or lost. In fact, there are others out there who've been brought to their knees, survived, and flourished, stronger and better than ever.

There is love and life after loss and break-up. It's yours to grab if you want it. Each chapter in this book is a different story. They won't be your story, but you will get a little something for yourself out of most, if not all.

After the Shared Stories, tackle the Self-Reflection exercises offered in Section 3. They are designed to help you start to navigate from where you are now, to where you want to be. The main message you'll learn in this book is that you have to know what you're about, what your own Personal Values are, in order to be able to gauge if potential suitors are right for you. Sounds simple? … Not getting this right is a common cause of failed relationships.

This book is intended to give you a sense of community and friendship. Get ready for helpful, practical ideas for taking control of your future.

I wish every reader hope and encouragement through the stories in this book.

## Contents

# Contents

# Is this book for me?

*Finding Love Again* is for people who have been in a long-term, committed relationship and it ended because of a break-up, or the death of one partner. It is for people aged over 30 years, and up to any age.

This book is for you if you *do* want to fall in love again.

**Circle your answers to this checklist.**

| | |
|---|---|
| I feel lonely. | Yes / No |
| I'm angry. | Yes / No |
| I'm not as confident as I would like to be. | Yes / No |
| I don't know where to go to meet people. | Yes / No |
| Online dating gives me the heebie-jeebies. | Yes / No |
| I've been hurt by friends' reactions to my situation. | Yes / No |
| I keep getting the same advice over and over. | Yes / No |
| I want to know how others handled their grief. | Yes / No |
| I feel that I've healed, but I haven't met anyone yet. | Yes / No |

If you answered yes to any of these questions, *Finding Love Again* is for you.

**Now answer these questions.**

I have insomnia. Yes / No

I feel that life isn't worth living anymore. Yes / No

I feel that people would be better off without me around. Yes / No

I feel worthless. Yes / No

I'm sick and rundown, and constantly tired. Yes / No

If you answered yes to any of these questions, I encourage you to continue reading *Finding Love Again* and also to seek out additional professional, in-person support. Sometimes we reach a point in life where a face-to-face connection is required. www.beyondblue.org.au is a great resource for exploring where you're at now, and who might be the best person for you to talk to. They have a Who Can Assist section that explains all of the health professions available (traditional and alternative) so you can decide which one would be the right one for you. If you prefer phoning, their number in Australia is 1300 224 636.

# Chapter 1

## Introduction to Finding Love Again

When I commenced the research phase for this book, I considered that I would interview couples in their second relationship to find out what they learned from their previous partnership, and why their second relationship was so much better because of what their past had taught them.

Well … it turned out that not everyone grew and learned from their experiences. Some people I interviewed had simply taken the first opportunity that came along because they were lonely, or, they looked for someone the opposite of the person they were with the first time around. This may be a mistake. For instance, someone who was with a violent man, might look only for a non-violent man ignoring other important qualities. A man who was with a woman who didn't find his jokes funny, might look for someone with the same sense of humour as him. This logic is understandable, but insufficient when it comes to building a harmonious, and satisfying relationship with longevity. It's important you have a holistic view of *all* the qualities that you're looking for in a new partner, not just one or two that your former partner didn't have. The people who approached finding a new partner based solely on what their previous partner didn't provide them, often found themselves in a new relationship with other – but just as many – problems.

Finding yourself single later in life is a different ball game than when you were in your twenties and falling in love for the first time. Now, at one end of the scale you look around and it feels like everyone you know is in a relationship. You have hardly any single friends, and the last thing you want to do is hang out at a pub to meet people. At the other end of the scale, you feel like everyone is dying around you, and most people want to sit at home doing nothing new! So where do you go to meet like-minded singles?

You may have heard online dating stories that make your stomach churn. It feels like all the 'good ones' are taken; the only people you're meeting seem to have endless amounts of 'baggage'. Plus, the rules have changed! Who calls who? Who pays? How long should you wait to reply to a text message? Should you text or call? Can women chase men now? Are there really more single women than men?

On top of all that, you're entering this new playground possibly with your confidence and personality suffering some dents. Your last relationship has left you reeling, perhaps nursing a broken heart, facing financial hardship, dealing with trust issues from betrayal, losing half your family and friends overnight, settling financial and custody arrangements with your ex-partner, moving or deciding whether to move or stay, dealing with lonely Sunday nights, or desperately missing someone you loved dearly who has passed away.

Many have travelled this road before you, and some of them share their stories with you in this book. The following chapters offer you companions with which to share your challenges and successes. Hindsight is a wonderful thing. May their openness and success help you on your path to your own clarity and new, ideal love relationship.

There is an old proverb – To know the road ahead, ask those coming back.

I'm a strong subscriber to modelling theory. When I see something or someone that impresses me, I think, "Good on you," and I admire and appreciate the work, dedication and commitment that I know that person put into achieving their goal – because, let's face it, nothing good comes easy. If I see something that I admire and truly want for myself, I engage with the person and find out what they did and how they did it. I learn from them.

This is what this book offers you. The following pages don't contain an instruction manual to finding love again – this is love after all, not a cake baking recipe. What they do offer you is information. Some information and tips from people who work in the relationships field, shared stories from people who have previously been where you are now, and shared stories from people who are where you are now. After you've had time to absorb and reflect what you read, at the end of the book, there are exercises to help you with your own healing and goal setting to set you on the path of getting you from where you are now to where you want to be, welcoming a new, successful, love relationship into your life. After reading this book and doing the exercises, you'll have created your own Action Plan for steps to finding love; steps that are applicable to you and your situation.

This is your chance to write your own story for what happens next. You decide the future direction that your life takes from this moment onward. That's exciting.

# What you'll find in *Finding Love Again*

**Section 1**

Relationship Theory – a short, easy-to-read section on leading research, key principles of successful relationships and how, based on this knowledge, you might approach dating to choose a partner right for you.

*Fact*

---

**Section 2**

Shared Stories – each story contains an introduction by the author, a person's story in the interviewee's voice, ending with discussion/evaluation and key points by the author.

*Opinion*

---

**Section 3**

Self-Reflection Exercises – exercises you can work through to reflect on your own love past and future, and create your personalised Action Plan for entering your ideal love relationship.

*Practical*

---

**Section 4**

Final Messages – some concluding thoughts about Releasing Your Past, Tips for Combating Loneliness and 7 Things You Need to Know Before You Date Again.

*The Holy Grail*

---

# Chapter 2

## Relationship Theory

Throughout the interviews for this book, it became evident that poor choices and poor communication were often prevalent in past failed relationships. For this reason, I've started the book with a snapshot of Relationship Theory. Just enough to focus you on the critical elements of successful relationships and direct you to excellent resources if you're interested in further reading or viewing. Now is a good time to learn more about critical success factors for healthy relationships so you know what you *do* and *don't* want in terms of how a prospective partner interacts with you. Some information may be new to you. Some information may be old, but give you a different perspective. All this knowledge will help you identify warning signs that a particular road could later bring you unhappiness. On the flip side, when the right person comes into your life, he or she is going to stand out from the pack because you'll recognise the signs.

I would like to introduce you to Mrs Robyn Donnelly, a Relationships Educator. Robyn has been delivering pre-marriage education to couples for 16 years, and is passionate about the science behind her work.

**Robyn, why should readers learn more about the key indicators of successful relationships?**

*As adults, we usually don't research things like this until we're in distress, and by then it's often too late. Knowing the principles of successful relationships arms us with knowledge that makes us more likely to choose our ideal partner. When looking for a new partner it's good to gain a better understanding of what makes a successful relationship so you can apply this knowledge early and not waste time on someone who isn't right for you.*

*Physical attraction is certainly important, but even more crucial, is ensuring that your most important Personal Values are aligned with your prospective partner.*

*It's important in relationships that both partners communicate well. Couples in good relationships often ask each other open-ended questions so they can 'check in' and truly know what the other person thinks and feels about things. Most of us do this when dating, when we're getting to know someone. But this can fall away into the mundane questions such as, "What's for dinner tonight?" in long-term relationships. Happy couples, twenty years in, still ask each other things such as, "What do you feel about where your career is at now?", or "How do you feel about our home, are there any changes you want to make?", or "What would be your ideal way to spend Christmas this year?" We all grow and change constantly. It's important that both partners understand this and take steps to remain connected at a deeper, more involved level.*

*Open-ended questions show genuine interest and allow you to truly know your partner. When dating, it's important that your date is asking you open-ended questions, thereby demonstrating a genuine interest in you, and that you're doing the same. This initial indicator can be a precursor to what you might expect later in the relationship.*

**How can we discover if a potential suitor's Personal Values are similar to ours?**

*Dating can be exhilarating and fun, but also horrifying or dull at times. You don't want to come across as wanting to jump immediately into a serious relationship, but you do want to get to know the person well enough to know if there is compatibility and potential there. Attraction and humour/fun are important, but there's more to it than that if you want success and longevity in a relationship. Here is a list of questions that you can slip into conversations to help you understand the Personal Values of the person you're getting to know. Become familiar with these questions, and use your discretion. Of course don't fire these questions at a person all at once. Ease them out over time in the course of getting to know someone.*

*Their answers will give you a greater understanding of your potential partner's Personal Values. There are no right and wrong answers to these questions; you're simply discovering whether their critical Personal Values are compatible to yours. The answers also give you real data to base your perceptions on, helping you to avoid the pitfall of reading a relationship through rose-coloured glasses.*

- *What type of relationship are you looking for?*
- *Tell me about your family.*
- *Have you always lived where you are now or have you moved around? What was that like?*
- *Are you a city person or country person at heart, and why?*
- *Who has influenced you most in life, and why?*
- *What qualities are you looking for in a new partner, and what qualities do you believe you bring to a relationship?*
- *When your eulogy is read what do you want people to say about you?*
- *What do you think makes a great relationship?*

- *What do you do to relax?*
- *What are you passionate about?*
- *What was the last really awesome day you had and what did you do?*
- *What would your ultimate night out with a date be like?*
- *What would your best holiday destination be, and why?*
- *What attributes do you have that are similar to your parents? Which ones are positive and which ones are negative?*
- *What do you do when you're stressed?*
- *What is one of your achievements that you're particularly proud of?*
- *Who can relax you when you're stressed, and how do they do it?*
- *What are you disappointed that you haven't done yet?*
- *What are ten things on your bucket list?*
- *What lessons have you learned in life that you hope your children wouldn't do?*
- *What are four Personal Values that you treasure in people?*
- *Who are the three people that you're most close to, and why are you close to them?*
- *What do you think of education in primary school and high school?*
- *Describe your ideal home; eg. is it big, small, messy, meticulous, homey, sparse?*
- *Describe the best Christmas you've ever had.*
- *Would you ever do charity work, and if you would, what would it be?*
- *When are you a planner and when do you go with the flow?*
- *How do you deal with conflict at work?*
- *How do you deal with conflict with friends?*
- *What makes you happy in a relationship?*
- *How important is sex to you?*

- *How important is money to you?*
- *How important is career to you?*
- *What is your ideal vision of work/life balance? Are you achieving this?*
- *What has been your biggest challenge in life and how did you handle it?*
- *Describe a relationship that you know of that works well. Why do you think it works so well?*

**Robyn, what are some indicators that a potential suitor isn't yet ready for a relationship?**

- *The obvious one, if they're trying to get their former partner back!*
- *If they have a lot of unresolved conflict.*
- *Someone who is 'I' focussed. For example, it's all about what they need for their own personal happiness with no consideration to anyone else.*

**What are some indicators that a potential suitor is not suitable for me?**

*If their major Personal Values don't match yours. For example, a deal breaker might be if you believe couples should create time to be alone and go on dates, but the other person thinks the bulk of your time should be spent hanging out with friends. Or vice versa, if you like to spend most of your time with your friends, but they don't.*

*Having similar views on the Personal Values is crucial, but this isn't something that you'll learn in a couple of dates. It takes time and shared experiences to get to know someone well enough to learn what their Personal Values are. When getting to know someone else it's important that you know what your own critical Personal Values are; those that are not negotiable for you, and those that are important to you but you have some room to negotiate. (This topic is explored further throughout this book).*

**Should you write a list of what you want in your next partner?**

*Yes. When you do your list, take some time to consider what your deal breaker Personal Values are and include them on your list. They will ultimately be the most important things you include.*

*Take care also not to write only those things that your former relationships didn't deliver for you. Also include the good things you've already experienced and enjoy in a relationship.*

# Shared Stories

The following first person narratives offer you multiple experiences from men and women who agreed to be interviewed to share with you how they healed after the death of a partner or a major break-up, and how they went on to fall in love again. Some even bravely agreed to be interviewed during their struggle, before healing and clarity. Due to the extreme personal nature of these stories, names and often places have been changed to protect people's identities. The photographs shown are models for illustrative purposes only.

The Shared Stories you are about to read are not recommendations of what you should or should not do. These stories are to stimulate your thinking, and for you to know that you are not alone. You might get a little from each story that personally resonates with you. You might disagree with some of the actions taken by some of the speakers. You might also disagree with some of the opinions expressed. That is all perfectly okay. This is a conversation, not a lecture. However, you will find, repeatedly, that the opinions and experiences expressed in the Shared Stories confirm the wide expanse of Relationship Theory that Robyn Donnelly summarised for you.

Everyone in this book hopes that you find balance, comfort and inspiration by reading their stories.

Following the Shared Stories, I encourage you to do the Self-Reflection Exercises designed to help you process your past and move confidently into your own future. These exercises have been included because during the interview phase, when I did interview people who were recently single, I usually later received emails from those interviewees along the lines of, "Thank you for hearing my story. Reading back what you wrote opened my eyes and is helping me to move on."

The Self-Reflection Exercises are designed to give you a similar opportunity to explore and analyse your personal story and your future.

This is an exciting time in your life; your chance to move thoughtfully towards your future. You have new wisdoms from your experiences and this book to use to your advantage.

The following shared stories are true and factual to the best of each interviewee's memory.

Names and places have been changed to protect people's identities.

**Photographs shown are models for illustrative purposes only to demonstrate gender and approximate ages of speakers. They are not the faces of the actual interviewees.**

# Chapter 3

## Ben's Story

**A 46-year-old Ambulance Officer, Ben talks about marrying young, divorce, and the experiences he's had along the way that showed him he used to 'play' the role of husband rather than being honest to himself.**

I had just turned 30 when my marriage broke up. I think it's normal for everyone to be obsessive about something after a major break-up. Some people choose sex, some drink, some drugs, some talk the ear off anyone who'll listen. I chose exercise. To centre myself, I went to the gym twice a day. Doing physical activity allowed me to be obsessive about something without wallowing. That was important to me.

I was 17-years-old when I met my first wife and we married when I was 23. I was a fairly reserved individual back then, having come from a strict Catholic upbringing. My father was a hard man from a long line of hard men. Back in the eighties, as a teenager discovering myself, I went through a stage where I had streaks in my hair. That was apparently a sign to my Dad that I was gay. He punched me a few times and said we didn't have homosexuals in our house. My Mum was dominant; she ran the family. I was close to my Mum. She died when I was 13.

Outwardly I look gregarious and energetic, but inside I'm a cautious person and have difficulty creating a bond with people. I left home at 18 years of age to forge my own life. I was searching for who I was. Back in the eighties I was quite innocent and I became a paramedic to save lives.

I met my first wife at a party. She pursued me through her brothers. It was difficult for my best friend because he had an enormous crush on her at the time, but she set her eyes on me, not him. She was blonde, buxom, and did some Page 3 type modelling for the local newspaper. In her mind she saw herself as a Penthouse Pet and quite the catch. My best friend thought she was fantastic. I was somewhat oblivious to all this.

She later told me that just before we got married, he came to our house and asked her if there was any chance for them. She answered the door in a towel. That's the way she tells the story. I know that he was very keen on her, and she did like attention. I'm prone to theatrics at times, so when she told me this I confronted him saying, "Judas sold his soul for thirteen pieces of silver, what was your price?" He was devastated.

Because of my upbringing, I was the type of man who would attach his wagon to something that wasn't quite right just to get along. I've since learned that that is living a shadow of yourself, rather than actually being yourself. There were moments in my marriage when I should have set boundaries, but I was still discovering myself and didn't do so. That's why now I talk about a journey of self-discovery. Because I wasn't true to myself back then, there came a time – later on – when I was suddenly forced to confront all the things that weren't right.

My wife and I both did very well in our careers. We mirrored our promotions quite closely and in hindsight, I would say that there was unhealthy competition between us. At one stage we were both studying and working and opportunities began opening up for each of us. My career started taking me away from home. I was driving two hours each way to get to work, and doing shift work.

In relationships, space can be a good thing, but it can also be a bad thing, especially if you're young and not being totally honest with each other and with yourselves. My wife started capitalising on that space. There was an uncomfortable moment when a guy turned up on my door to have what I would call a 'date' to go to the beach with my wife for the day. He was just as uncomfortable as I was. Rather than expressing to me that there were problems in our marriage, I think she expressed it to her male friends.

That was an unusual moment in our marriage for me to navigate through. In reflection, I should have insisted, "What is this all about?" I did ask, but she said, "None of your business" and I simply accepted that and we continued on with our charade.

There started to be talk of children. In the context of this, it's important for me to acknowledge that I wasn't being the perfect husband. I wasn't providing her with what she needed. Whether it was too much attention or not enough, I'm not sure. Whatever it was, I clearly wasn't right for her. I didn't want to have children because there was a strong familial link to mental illness in her family, plus I wasn't feeling responsible enough myself at the time to be a father.

We went overseas for a month-long holiday and on day two I could tell she was missing someone, and that someone clearly wasn't me because I was there!

We had an emotional and explosive conversation – but we didn't cry, which in reflection was a bad sign. We talked about what we should do. In my view I was overseas and I wanted to finish my holiday so we did, but it was uncomfortable and we slept in separate beds.

Back home we went our separate ways. I went out and proactively initiated divorce proceedings. I don't think she expected me to do that because her behaviour became unusual in that she started to cry a lot. We were still in the same house, but the space was insurmountable to come back from. I was cordial, but perhaps also clinical and cold – it shocked her I think. I wasn't rude, saying, "Thank you, I appreciate the memories", but I was process driven.

The dividing of property was bitter. We had a lot of things from a physical perspective but her Mum and Dad had given us a leg up in the beginning and she had received an inheritance from an aunt while we were together. My view was that we should have split everything 50/50. Her view was 90% for her and 10% for me. She basically said that her family was so wealthy that she would take me to court until she won. I sought legal advice, and was told that at the end of the day it might not be worth the fight and it could take a long time, so I took the 10%. I don't regret this, but my new wife does. At the time, I just wanted to move on. I wasn't overly surprised by the turn of events; there had always been a strong, nasty streak in her. During our marriage I used to tease her about her self-interest, and her attitude of 'I am woman, hear me roar.'

Looking back, some form of disruption in our lives can be a good thing because it opens up the space to think, 'Is this me, or do I need to change something about myself?' When I was younger, I didn't have the maturity to step outside and see all this and do something about it. Honesty – truth to yourself and your own nature – is important. Part of who I have become now is about naval gazing. Young people can sometimes get together, follow along the script, and not necessarily be truly honest. I wasn't true to myself during my first marriage. My first instinct was to avoid conflict. I wasn't a person who could have confrontation without it being negative. If I had been honest with myself, I never would have accepted it that day my wife said, "It's none of your business." Partners can't say that something that happens in their lives is none of your business! At the time, I should have asked myself, "Is this my life, or is this the theatre of my life?" Because I was still living the theatre, I didn't have the confidence to pursue the question.

I think we can all look back through our own personal development, and that of our close friends, and see that there are times that we get locked into a stage, and other times when we evolve quite rapidly. You can get locked into a period that isn't right, but lack the ability to transition out of it. Some form of disruption has to occur – whether it's positive or negative – something has to occur to cause you to self-reflect. You don't want to constantly self-reflect or you'll never do anything, but you need disruption to prompt you, at times, to re-evaluate your model.

Disruption can be good even though the root cause may be bad. Going through my divorce was horrendous, yet it's probably the best thing that's ever happened to me. I went to the gym, read and reflected. I got a chance to pack everything into place in my head. If you asked the people at work, where the role I play is boss to many people, they would tell you that I'm an extrovert. In my private life, I'm an introvert. The reflection was exactly what I needed at that point in time.

Losing half my friends and family overnight was very hurtful because I'm so slow to bring people in. Losing people in an instant and having nothing to replace it with, is very hard, there's no doubt about that.

As a single bloke I didn't chat to many of my mates about what I was going through. I only chatted to one who had himself been married for years. He sort of helped me normalise it. I'm a social person, but I'm also very comfortable in my own company so I wasn't lonely while I was single. However, I'm also the type of person who needs another. I certainly experienced the shock of finding myself single at 30 years of age. It was quite different than being single as a teenager. But I wasn't in desperate search of company. I knew I needed to find out what I was about. Even though I said earlier that I was clinical in my approach to our break-up, it was still difficult emotionally, and the financial disintegration was hard.

I think most of us have a 'wild' portion of time when we go through a break-up, but wild for me is probably tame for most people. I socialised with one friend, going out to the clubs. I didn't overdo the drinking because I'm a health conscious person. My obsession became exercise. I was tempted, like everyone I guess, to fall into 'woe is me, why is all this happening to me?' but I didn't want to do that, and obsessing about the gym helped me manage those feelings.

At the gym, I ran into a lady who had in the past looked after our dogs when we went overseas. When Lisa had looked after our dogs, I wasn't attracted to her – I just don't think like that when I'm not available. But I did think she was a nice person. Running into her again, once I *was* available, I noticed how attractive she was. Our friendship developed over the next few months at the gym, until one of the instructors asked me out on a date. The instructor wasn't comfortable with it being just her and I though, so she invited her friend Lisa along and the three of us ended up out at dinner.

Over the course of the night, Lisa and I had a really good time together. When we were leaving, I almost kissed Lisa goodbye because the attraction was strong. The instructor recognised that Lisa and I made a great couple and encouraged us to be together.

I suppose I had plenty of attention while I was single but I wasn't interested in anything trivial. I don't do one-night stands, and I wasn't interested in being with someone to fill in time. However, I soon realised Lisa was a good person and somebody I wanted to be with. We had great conversations. I knew it was right because I felt good letting her inside and sharing myself with her. I waited to kiss her until I was absolutely sure that she was the one for me, and then our relationship grew from there. We were good for each other. We shared lots of laughs, and had similar senses of humour.

We also had opportunities to have conflict with each other, and whereas in the past I did everything I could to avoid conflict in my relationship, now I see it as a good thing. I embraced it. In the past I would compromise myself to avoid conflict, whereas with Lisa I've learned that I need to express myself differently. We've had many healthy debates and even arguments where we've expressed ourselves. It's normal to have different points of view and argue and come through it to the other side. If you're in a relationship and there's no arguing, one of you in the relationship isn't being true to themself.

I've certainly matured for my second relationship. We're both quick to air and protect our point of view, but we're also both mature enough to know that we're not always right.

When Lisa and I first moved in together, it was relatively seamless in terms of our value systems. We had the same ideas about how we keep house, and similar ideas about 'together' time and 'alone' time. We were good friends, as well as lovers, and it was quite natural and smooth. I have friends who've moved in with their partner and then found that they have completely different Personal Values around the house. This can be quite scary for people. A simple analogy – they feel like they're navigating the streets in America instead of Australia. Each time they go to cross the road they look the wrong way because everyone else is driving on the wrong side of the road. It can be like that for some people moving in together – everything looks the same, but in fact, it's opposite. This is just one more reason why it's so important to explore each other's Personal Values before jumping into a relationship.

I felt more at home with Lisa than I ever did in my first marriage, because with Lisa I had learned to be honest.

Lisa and her family are loud and expressive. That took a bit of getting used to for me. As I guess you can imagine by now – I'm a quiet person. The first time I met her family all they did was fight. Lisa ended the night by saying, "You've all embarrassed me and I never want to see you again!" She's very close to her family; they got over it quickly. They were an eye-opener for me. They're unlike any other family I've ever met. They have a lot of healthy conflict. They all speak their mind, but they never dwell on anything. It's been good for me to be exposed to this way of operating.

Of course, I always knew Lisa had a daughter. Before entering into a relationship with her I had to put a lot of thought into whether or not I wanted to be a part of something that came from another part of her life. I never wanted children, but when your love grows for someone, and a child is part of that person you're in love with, you can't separate from that. You've got to be willing to accept the ex-husband into your life because he's a part of that child too. That was probably the hardest part for me to accept initially. The former me would have found that too hard. The new, more mature Ben had to come to terms with that if I wanted Lisa: it was Lisa, Sam and Damien! In practice this was all difficult for me. I'm good with kids who are in my life for short periods, but I'm actually not that good with a kid who is in my presence 24 hours a day. It's hard enough to bring two views together to raise a child – we had to bring four views together (including Lisa's ex-husband and his new partner).

I wasn't part of Sam's life until she was six. I had to accept that there were things happening in her upbringing that I didn't necessarily agree with, but I couldn't just plonk in and say, "No, I don't like it that way, things are going to happen my way from now on."

In the beginning, I wasn't natural with Sam. In fact, I was aloof. For instance, snot probably grossed me out when it shouldn't have. It took me time to get used to those things. Lisa, Sam and I weren't fighting, it just took me a couple of years to get used to having a child around, and to learn how to manage it. I'm more comfortable now being part of a blended family, but there is continuous management in that because I can't just think about myself and my own family; there is another family involved as well – Sam's father's family.

I first met Sam's father, Damien, at a drop-off. We simply introduced ourselves and shook hands. One day in particular stands out to me because it prompted me to think how I should respond if things ever escalated. On this day, Lisa and Damien were having a dust-up about something to do with Sam. Lisa gave Damien a gob-full. It was interesting to watch Lisa passionately ripping into someone else! I didn't know how Damien was going to respond to it, but he just took it. I was left wondering what my role should be if he did arc up back at her.

I have actually played the role of peacemaker between Lisa and Damien a couple of times since then, but overall, we never really have any major issues with Damien. Ultimately, the motivation for all of us is Sam. When you're a blended family it's challenging enough, without fighting as well. We get Christmas presents for their new child. Sam is in a blended family – she has no choice in that. As the adults in her life, it's our job to make it as functional as possible for her. Damien is an excellent father. We've had complex discussions around schooling, and how Sam talks and acts at our house and at their house; eg. food choices, sport, hobbies, jobs. Damien and his wife approached us asking that Sam spend a week with them and then a week with us. It's working well. They asked Lisa to write up all the rules that she wanted to be maintained consistently across both homes. Lisa did that and then they all communicated with each other about it and included rules such as:

- Never bag the other parents
- Respect for teachers
- Be grateful for what you've got.

Ultimately, we all want consistency for Sam. None of us are perfect; there are definitely challenges along the way, but as far as blended families go, we're pretty good.

**What have you learned about relationships?**

First and foremost, be true to yourself. To contrast my current marriage to my previous one, I wasn't myself in my first marriage. At the time, I didn't realise that by accommodating my internal need to avoid conflict, I compromised myself to keep the peace. When the crisis point came, it came to teach me that important lesson. The strength in my current marriage is that I've learnt that conflict done in the right way is a good thing; it helps to re-energise and re-frame what the relationship is all about. That's one of the great things about Lisa; she's very conscious of who she is and what she will and won't stand for. At the same time, she's great at talking things through. We have healthy, robust conversations.

There's always been a dichotomy between me in my personal and work lives. In private, I'm reluctant to reveal truths. Lisa has made me realise that when you're with a partner it's important to share those things with the person you love so you can work on your relationship together.

I'm from the cusp of the generation where men don't cry and emotion is a weakness. It took a long time to overcome those mental barriers and to see that talking about your feelings is important. Going back to my previous marriage, it wasn't fair to my first wife that she saw a reflection of me, instead of the real me. Lisa has been great for me. For her, silence isn't an answer. To be drawn into those types of conversations was difficult for me at first; but Lisa just did it. She's an engaging person and she brings it out in people. She'll always tell me what she's thinking, and then she'll ask me what I think about it too, and I'm engaged to answer. At work, I now use communication skills she's taught me at home.

The second thing I've learnt about relationships, is to make sure you really know the person you're about to enter into a relationship with. We're all in many respects guilty of this; we go by what someone looks like when we first meet them. There'll always be that component of physical attraction first, but then the key, I think, is to get to know the Personal Values of that person, and the boundaries they set around themselves, and then make sure the two of you are compatible. My first wife was attractive, but our critical Personal Values were different. Ultimately, it's the mental connection that is the real strength.

Unpacking 'getting to know yourself' is a complex piece of work, so the third thing I learned was to not jump too soon into a relationship. I got married very young, and as a consequence didn't know who I was. I didn't know what I was about, but more importantly, I didn't know what I wasn't about.

When thinking of getting married, we must test our motivation, and test it again, because it's a big commitment and there are plenty of ways to screw it up. I think everybody has a little voice that sits inside their gut (as opposed to their head) and it tends to provide instinctual rather than intellectual advice. I think we should listen to that – not to the point of paralysis – but certainly hear what our gut is saying to us. With Lisa, I was hypersensitive to what my gut was telling me, and my instinct was telling me it was all good. That's why I married Lisa and now we've just had our ten-year anniversary. We've had an interesting, tumultuous and passionate relationship, and it's full of love and longevity.

**Do the rules change at ten years? How do you keep it interesting?**

The broad boundaries are consistent but the details change. If you keep doing what you've always done, don't be surprised when you keep getting what you've always got. As you grow, you change, as does your partner. If you keep following the same rules as you did ten years ago, you'll find they're not applicable to the now. Lisa and I are good at talking about that. In my first marriage, I was self-deluded and disconnected. I just wanted a snapshot of rules that fit everything. Lisa and I have boundaries about what we will and won't accept, and within those boundaries we talk things through. If you stubbornly start doing things your own way, that space can become disconnected quickly.

I don't like it when couples pick on each other. For instance, you might hear a guy always saying he doesn't get enough sex. I think human beings are creatures of habit. You are what you repeatedly do, whether you like it or not. If you repeatedly talk your partner down in front of others, even if you think you're joking – which I think you're not – you're going to be affecting your partner. You're knocking someone else down to build yourself up; getting a laugh from the crowd. Ultimately you're winning at the expense of someone else and even if they don't have the strength to tell you, you're hurting them. I think this kind of behaviour opens up the space to then start being disrespectful in other ways. I'm not saying you can never banter in your relationship; that can be fun. There are plenty of ways of having fun without putting your partner down.

**What is your take on modern relationships?**

There are no longer male roles and female roles – there are 'family' roles. With both partners usually working full-time now, the traditional roles of our parents no longer hold true. I know the second I slip up and say to Lisa that I'm "helping out" around the house, that I've pushed a button. I've moved past the notion that I'm helping out, and have come to acknowledge that I'm actually just doing my share.

One of the key lessons I've learnt is that the things for myself in my daily routine need to be focussed on last. Let me explain that more. As nurturers, women will always look after everyone else first. If Lisa and I tackle the 'family' tasks together, but she focuses on everyone else first (eg. kids' dinners, lunches for the next day, homework, ironing, etc.) but I focus on my things first (my own lunch, my own sports gear, etc.) by the time I go to help Lisa she's already done everything for the kids so there's nothing left for me to do. I've found that by changing my rhythm and first focusing on the 'family' tasks and then my own, that we have a happy, peaceful life because that matches the woman's rhythm. Really, it makes no difference to me in the long run to look after the kids first and then get my own gear sorted. The feeding, homework, cleaning and preparation in a family is a production that happens day in and day out. When it comes to children, you can't indulge in self-pity or say that you're tired. When both partners work full-time, it's simply not fair to leave the bulk of the responsibility to the woman in the relationship simply because she's female. In the 21st century you both have to work because you want to live a certain lifestyle, so you have to re-contextualise *everything* at home so you are both equally responsible for *all* the home requirements.

If you're a guy and wondering why your partner isn't jumping around in lingerie think about all the noise that's in her head just to get herself and the kids and you out of the house in the morning. If you want your wife to be happy, support her in the house, be there when she needs you, and equally contribute to the kids. If you can do that you'll reduce the noise in her head and she'll have more time to think about you. If you don't do those things, don't be surprised when your wife's mind isn't 'on it'. Even if you don't have a wife like mine who tells you what she's thinking and feeling, you'll still have a wife who thinks this way.

Lisa and I goal-set together. We talk about our family goals and our personal goals. I think it's important to do that. If you don't know where you're going, how will you know when you get there? We talk about this a lot. It's one of the things that's helped us to stay on focus with each other.

I guess that one last thing to mention about modern family life is how important it is to connect with each other's families. Not having compatibility amongst the extended family can be difficult. Ultimately, if there's little harmony, someone is going to have to compromise, whether it's them or you or your partner. When someone has to compromise, that opens up the opportunity for gaps to start appearing.

# Author's Notes

Ben thoughtfully unpacked his break-up and planned his future. A strength that helped Ben to come out on top in life was that he wasn't lonely while he was single. Loneliness can lead one to accept situations that aren't ideal, including becoming involved in a relationship that is 'acceptable', rather than 'joyful'. Are you worthy of a joyful relationship? Of course you are!

Loneliness is a real threat after you've had someone by your side for years and overnight they, their family and many of your mutual friends are ripped from your life. Some singles get stuck in the pain of losing friends and the ex-partner's family. However, it happens to most people after a break-up. Accept it as a fact of life. Cherish your good memories with people, and don't resent them if they fade away. Your break-up affects others too, not just you. Let those who need to move on, do so. There will always be different people in your life for different stages. It's all perfectly normal, and perfectly okay.

If you're lonely, get into the habit of planning your week in advance. When are you alone? What can you do to fill that time? Who is available and interested in the same things that you are? What groups or organised activities are available in your local community?

# Key Points From Ben's Chapter

1. Be clear about your Personal Values. You need to rediscover not only what you are about, but also what you aren't about.
2. Choose a healthy 'obsession' or 'focus' to keep occupied; eg exercise, travel, meditation, art, etc. What's your passion? Make that your focus.
3. Reflect on your previous relationship and identify what you did well, and what you could improve on.

# Chapter 4

## Jade's Story

**Jade admits that when she found herself single after a 12-year relationship she struggled as a 32-year-old single woman. Her struggle shocked her. She didn't see it coming.**

Yesterday I was sitting out on my back deck reading a book while my husband worked on his laptop in a nearby room. I could see him through a window. I like looking at him – his nearness makes me feel secure and content. It's only recently that I've come to value the word: *contentment*. When I look back through thc past seven years, which is when I first met him, it amazes me how far I've journeyed out of my comfort zone. I look back through my life and see two streamers fanned out behind me – one containing wise decisions, laughter, great times, adventures, awesome people, quite startling achievements that I'm proud of; the other streamer contains a series of train wrecks – some small in scale, one so huge it changed the core of who I am as a human being. Both streamers flap in the wind together; interwoven to create one story. I often wonder if everyone feels that way … that life is a series of achievements and stuff-ups; some things we're proud of, others we're not. Despite my best intentions, at times my level of wisdom hadn't yet caught up with the experiences of the moment and I made bad decisions. Knowing that mistakes are part of being human doesn't always alleviate the sting.

There's a saying I like: 'Home is where our story begins.' My sister died when she was 36-years-old. I was just 28. She was beautiful and vivacious and I still think about her every day. Now, at 42, I'm a big believer that we only get one crack at this life and we don't know how long or short we're going to be here for. I'm driven to fulfil all my dreams and experience everything I can. I regularly say to myself, "You're only here once, what is your wildest desire right now?" I have an innate belief that I can do or achieve anything I truly want so long as I'm prepared to put in the hard work. This quality arrived in my DNA courtesy of my Dad. I have found, though, that doing lots of things doesn't automatically make you happy.

My parents were old school. There were times when I looked at friends whose parents were far more lenient than mine, or who bought their kids their first car, etc., and I thought, "Wow, that would be cool." Now, looking back, I thank my parents for allowing me the chance to struggle at times – because struggle makes us who we are.
My parents raised us with good morals, a strong work ethic, and good money sense. Dad passed away in 2007 – he was always up for a laugh, and was wise; he liked to orate on the perils of the rich getter richer and the poor getting poorer. Mum taught me how to grow an investment portfolio of rental properties to ensure my independence. She liked to warn me of the dangers in the world, encourage me to save money, and keep a clean house. When it came to confidence in my opinions, who I am as a woman and my self-worth of how I should expect to be treated by other people, there wasn't any of that – just as there wasn't in her generation. Humility was admired and encouraged. Growing up, I was expected to be seen and not heard. Despite being dux of Grade 10, I was made to leave school at the end of that year because I didn't need Grade 12 or a tertiary education to be a secretary in the public service, which is

what my parents felt I should do. I'm not criticising my parents. I love them both very much. I'm articulating how my experiences shaped me because I had to later come to understand what I was good at, and where I lacked appropriate skills.

Looking back, I can see that throughout my life I've underestimated the worth of myself, particularly my worth as a partner. I've never expected much, demanded even less, and quietly waited for people to see and appreciate the gem inside. It took me many years to learn to speak up for myself in some situations. Don't get me wrong, I'm not a serial introvert. Sometimes I'm an introvert, and sometimes an extrovert. I'm human.

**My First Relationship**

I met my first serious partner when I was 21-years-old. We dated for four years at which time we were out for a drive one day, saw an acreage block for sale on top of a hill, loved it, and bought it. He and I weren't big on serious conversations. We were all about the fun, and we had lots of it – four wheel driving, camping, jet skiing, trail bike riding – and after we bought our block, fabulously funny and adrenalin fuelled times with the neighbours. We got together to fell and burn enormous trees on our acreages, hire u-drive bobcats to do our own earthworks, make potato launchers that we would shoot into the bush, and all manner of exciting things you can do out on land. My first partner was a strong Aussie bloke, fun to be around, and a magnet to like-minded people. We were a good match because I have a fair amount of tomboy in me. There was only one thing marring my happiness at the time. After we built our house and were ready to move in together, I raised my first conversation with him about marriage and discovered he didn't believe in it. He thought it was just a piece of paper. I was devastated – marriage means the world to me. Friends can come and go; family have no choice in the matter. On the other hand, marriage, to me, is choosing someone to be your family for life – what a beautiful acknowledgement of the depth of your love for another human being.

We got engaged because it was important to me, but as time wore on I felt empty at his lack of emotional investment in marrying me and I stopped wearing the ring. He didn't say anything when I did so. In my mind, I preferred to wait until he was ready to get married. I loved him very much and I wanted the moment that I walked down the aisle to him to be perfect. I pictured the moment our eyes would meet midway through my walk towards him, and I wanted his eyes to be sparkling with happiness. I wanted that, or nothing. I was idealistic, naïve, unrealistic. I chose to wait; never expressing to him the beautiful picture I had in my mind. He was very good, and fun of course, with kids – we both were – so I figured there would come a time when he would want kids of his own and he'd want to get married to consolidate our family. Streetwise in some ways, tough in some ways, I was also naïve in my twenties. A wiser woman would have talked more to her partner, and raised the topic of having a family, even told her partner of the dream she had of their sparkling eyes meeting midway down the aisle. I didn't. I lacked appropriate communication skills to calmly acknowledge and convey my needs and desires. Instead, I swept things under the carpet and continued playing practical jokes, laughing, playing house, and adventure seeking with him. For the last three years of our relationship, once a year, for some inexplicable reason – every Easter holidays – I would raise the topic of marriage. It never went well. I was hopeless at communicating appropriately about the topic, always becoming tearful and emotional. He would tell me to stop nagging him.

I was blissfully happy in one sense, soulfully hurting on another. I started to doubt myself and became insecure. Why did he not want to marry me? Was I not good enough? My self-doubt grew as time went on. Looking back, I put him on a pedestal. Perhaps I admired him too much. Women need their men strong. We like to look up to our partner and know that we can depend on them in any situation, small or big, to be calm, brave and know the right thing to do. I guess that most likely, men like their women to be strong too – keep them on their toes. Ever heard of the book *Why Men Marry Bitches*? After my partner left me, my Mum gave me that book. I think she may have been trying to tell me something. I have since come to understand how wrong it was of me to assume that one day he would simply change his mind about his core Personal Value about marriage. That was silly on my part.

**The day that changed our lives**

On 21 July, 2000 I received the phone call that changed me, and everyone in my family. The phone call came very early in the morning, I can't tell you exactly when, but I was still asleep. My now former partner had already left for work; he left at 4.30am. When my brother's and sister-in-law's words on the other end of the phone actually sunk into me I tried to speak but words wouldn't come out of my mouth. A basal, animalistic noise emanated instead. My sister and brother-in-law had been murdered during the night in front of their seven kids. I hung up the phone. I wasn't crying. My body was too deep in shock for such a normal response. I phoned my partner's mobile. I still couldn't speak – only the animal sounds came out – like a dingo caught in a steel trap. My partner later told me he immediately knew it was something horrific so he turned on the radio and heard that there had been a double homicide and that it was in the town that my sister lived in. My sister and brother-in-law had been married for two years, and for both of them this was their second union. My sister had two children from her previous relationship. My brother-in-law had five children from his previous marriage. Both were experiencing extremely difficult times with their former partners. My partner at the time had a bad but hardly believable feeling that it was them when he heard the news of the homicide. He sensed that I would go to my parents' house so he drove straight there.

My parents lived 25 minutes from our house. I'm not sure how I made that trip on my own. I put on jeans, brushed my teeth and hair, and got in my car and drove. I didn't speed, I didn't cry, the only sign of trauma was my shaking body. When I arrived at my parents' house my Mum was sitting at the kitchen table. Dad was sitting in a chair about 2m away from her. Neither were crying, although you could see that Mum had been. Neither were speaking. They were both grey, and much, much older than when I had seen them the previous day. I walked through the door and none of us said a word. We looked at each other, our eyes sharing a world of pain. I walked past them and leant on the kitchen bench. My oldest sister arrived. She said, "I can't believe it" and then she too stood apart and was simply still. My brother arrived. He didn't say anything. All five of us were very deeply in shock. We stood apart … not touching … not speaking, but sharing each other's pain. My partner arrived. People began moving, silently comforting each other. My brother's wife arrived, and people began crying and talking.

We had to travel three hours to go to the police station in the town where my sister and brother-in-law were killed. The police station was where my seven nieces and nephews were being cared for. My Mum, Dad, oldest sister, my partner and myself drove there. My partner did what he had to do to help us do what we needed to do – getting petrol, directions, etc. – things that my family and I simply couldn't absorb into our minds at the time. We were oblivious to much around us, all deep in shock. When we arrived at the police station we were ushered inside a small room and a detective explained what happened by drawing the rooms of my sister's and brother-in-law's house on a sheet of paper and showing us with small marks who was killed where and how. When you're in shock your body shuts down on you, compartment by compartment, leaving only those necessary elements you need to breathe and walk, etc, in working order. You're not capable of complex emotions or comprehension. All I heard was, "Your sister was shot here, she ran here, and died here." Those words ran over and over and over in my head and I wasn't aware of anything else around me. Outwardly I showed little reaction.

My sister had a gorgeous smile, dancing eyes and huge dimples. She was beautiful and vivacious inside and out. She was a great mother. I couldn't comprehend how anyone could have killed her. I simply couldn't take it in. Looking back, I can remember how my mind shut down into cordoned off compartments in response to shock. It's amazing how the mind physically protects itself from things it can't handle.

I don't like making the murders a story. Their lives, their beautiful natures, their kids, their parents, their siblings, their friends, the impact they left on so many – it is far too important and too profound for me to turn it into entertainment. These are memories that need to be respected and treasured – shared in person amongst people who love and care for each other, and loved and cared for my sister and brother-in-law. Years ago, with my parents' blessing, I agreed to a magazine interview because we wanted to convey our belief that 'life' sentences should mean actual life, and not 15 years, in sentencing murderers. However, when I saw the magazine in the shops and the cover shouted in capital letters *A Man Shot My Sister*, I was mortified by the sensationalist commercialism applied to my sister's story. Please bear with me while I share only what is relevant to the topic of this book.

It turned out that a good friend of mine was a police officer at the station we drove to. When we arrived at the police station she saw me walk in with my family and in a moment of clarity realised that the murder victim was my sister. She explained our relationship to her boss and asked to be tasked with looking out for my family in those first few agonising days. She organised a motel for us and looked out for us in ways that I was oblivious to at the time. For instance, at one time she and I walked to the local corner store to get tea and coffee. I later found out that when we entered the shop, the assistant and some customers were discussing the murders and their ill-informed opinions about it. I didn't realise, walking in to the back of the shop to look for tea. My police officer friend, out of my sight, held her badge up (she was in civvies) and discreetly told them to shush. This was just one of a thousand things she did while we weren't functioning well. My partner also played a similar role for our family. Months later, when I thanked my friend, she told me that they were excruciating days and she didn't think she could have got through them without my partner. She said he was solid; a tower of strength. For the first two weeks following the murders, my partner was absolutely wonderful, strong. That's the kind of man he was.

Two weeks after the tragedy we held an emotional double funeral and my partner returned to work. At this time we'd been together for nine years. For many years afterwards it tortured me how our near perfect relationship disintegrated during the three years following the funeral. Looking back now, ten years later, I think I understand. I made mistakes, and he made mistakes. During my relationship I was oblivious to the ramifications of some of my actions and decisions.

My most profound lesson from my first relationship was our inferior communication skills. For much of our relationship we were so busy having fun that we didn't talk about the big stuff. We were Aussies and Aussies don't wallow. You did what you had to do to get on. I didn't express my needs to him, and he didn't express his needs to me. This served us well for nine years in good times. Over the next three years, in the hard times following the deaths and subsequent court cases, it eventually resulted in our break up … I think.

Over the next two years, I attended every day of every trial, determined that my sister and brother-in-law were not going to be reduced to mere "female victim" and "male victim" in the courtroom. They were very much loved, and there was no way I wasn't going to be there for them. What I heard and saw in those courtrooms changed the essence of who I am as a human being. My partner only ever took one day off work to go to court, so he didn't experience the dual horror and boredom of courtrooms with me. He didn't experience what it was like to sit and watch the killer, to see the gun for the first time, to hear everyone talk so clinically about my sister's and brother-in-law's final moments. And I didn't come home and talk about it much. Partly from exhaustion, partly because I knew my partner wanted to go on living as 'normally' as possible.

Before the murders, I used to think that if anyone ever raped or killed someone I loved, that I would kill them. It's a throwaway line we use to make sense of the world. When my sister was murdered, I desperately struggled with the impotent feeling of helplessness. Real life isn't like in the movies where the loved ones get to take action, or to solve the case and apprehend the killer. In real life, you're pushed to the side so the police can conduct the investigation. It becomes a crime against the State, not a crime against your family. You're told to go home and get on with your own life – which is an impossibility. I struggled with feelings of intense dislike towards myself because I allowed someone to kill my sister, and I wasn't doing anything about it – I didn't even yell at her killer when I did see him. I just stood and watched, words inadequate to convey what was inside me.

Impotently doing nothing had a devastating effect on my personality. I no longer recognised, nor liked, who I was. My Personal Values had been shattered out of the water, and I was reeling. I no longer believed there was some good in everyone; we had been touched by pure evil, which previously I didn't really believe existed. And contrary to throw away lines from the past, I was not the 'hero' I imagined. At the time, I felt pathetic, inadequate, weak and dishonourable to my sister's memory.

There's a Jodie Foster movie called *The Brave One* in which her partner is murdered. When someone asks her, "How do you pull it back together?", her character replies, "You don't. You become someone else … a stranger." It's a good way to describe it. My new personality contained revulsion for the impotent part of me that stood by and did nothing, hate for the killer, and a mind portioned into two separate parts so that the ugliness of the killer couldn't wrap itself around the beauty that was my sister. I kept memories of my sister and the reality of her killer completely separate in my head, refusing to rob her of any more than he already had.

These things I've shared in the last few paragraphs are thoughts I didn't share with anyone; not even my partner.

After two years of insomnia and legal trials I developed clinical depression and was forced to take six months off work. Initially, I was terribly embarrassed to have depression, seeing it as a weakness. I came to understand, after much convincing by doctors and a psychologist, that it was a legitimate medical condition caused by chemical changes in my body due to prolonged shock and sleep deprivation. This was a journey I made alone. My partner and I didn't talk about it. I don't really know what he thought of my depression, but I suspect he saw me as weak at the time. I spent weeks curled up in the foetal position on the floor, crying, and when I knew he was coming home I'd get up, shower, cook dinner and try to act like nothing was wrong. I now suspect my acting was highly unsuccessful and that he most likely felt like he was living with the shell of his former girlfriend. At the time I thought I was doing the right thing by him by trying to pretend that life was normal.

As treatment for my depression started working, I began looking around at the world outside the pain inside my own head. I realised I didn't feel close to my partner anymore. I tried talking to him about it, asking him if he was happy. At the time, he said yes, but after a few more conversations and a couple of fights (which we previously didn't do), we decided that perhaps we should have a counselling session together. However, before we got there, we had a tiff in the car on the way to see a movie and he ended our relationship by saying, "I'm not in love with you anymore, I'm leaving." We drove home and he left straight away, never giving me any greater explanation than that. We amicably divided our twelve years together, and that was that. Still struggling with depression, I now slipped into low self-esteem as well. I couldn't understand how someone I loved so deeply and for so long, could just leave me like that. Was I really that horrible, that weak? Was our whole 12 years together a joke? I had never had low self-esteem before. I now have a much greater appreciation of how debilitating it is.

Everyone handles break-ups differently. I'm not proud of the way I handled mine. Actually, I'm proud of some things. I handled many things with dignity, particularly the dividing of money and property. My ex-partner and I were fair and reasonable with each other. We didn't get our families involved, and we treated each other with respect. I'm proud of the way I was resourceful and got boarders into the house to help with the mortgage so that I could afford to stay living on my acreage property. And I'm proud of the way I worked hard and continued to grow my business despite the pain I was in. Three things I'm not proud of are:

1. The way I retreated into myself and didn't talk about what was going on inside me.
2. That I basically got drunk for the first six months. I couldn't handle thinking, so every night I got drunk and partied instead. A couple of people said to me, "Jade, is this really the way to handle this?" and I would laugh and reply along the lines of, "Hell yes, when I'm ready to think about things, I'll stop drinking."
3. That I couldn't stand being on my own so I lost sight of my morals and dated and/or slept with some guys who I shouldn't have – which just made me feel worse about myself. I couldn't even stand going grocery shopping by myself so I would either eat meat and veg at the pub, grab take out, or on the rare occasion that I actually went grocery shopping, I would borrow a neighbour's kid to come with me for company.

None of my friends were single; most had small children and couldn't go out much, and my best friends lived interstate. I was lonely and had lost sight of who I was. In my quest to drink my way through the pain I wasn't being true to myself or my core Personal Values, and I'm not particularly proud of the person I was during that period of time. I was weak, lonely and desperately struggling as a mid-thirties single person. I found it quite shocking to discover that some men stereotyped me as someone who needed to get married quickly because my biological clock was ticking. I found this rather absurd and disconcerting. I felt like I'd gone from prime rib fillet in my twenties to ordinary old chuck steak in my thirties. I was annoyed that society made me feel that way. I wasn't suicidal, but I did, at times, feel like life would be better if I could just die.

A cousin reached out to me, and it was the beginning of me finding myself again. I started walking with her three times a week after work, and for months we talked and talked and talked – about her and me. I could feel her strength rubbing off on me in shades as I gradually healed and found my former personality and confidence – the girl I truly was. I'm a friend who is always there for her friends, but I'm also someone who finds it difficult to ask for help when I personally need it. My cousin saw through that and made a real effort to give me consistent energy and love at the lowest point in my life. She has a very special place in my heart.

I also sought the assistance of some alternative therapies – hypnotherapy and kinesiology – and found them helpful in releasing emotional blockages and enabling the restoration of normal sleep patterns.

As I became stronger, I compiled a list of what I wanted in my future partner. I wanted to find my equal. Someone who was successful in their career, had strong family values, believed in marriage, enjoyed having fun but was also responsible, didn't smoke, had a strong social conscience, and was loyal, caring and a nice person. It still amuses me how 'nice' and 'responsible' are the last qualities we seek in a partner when we're young, but how important these two qualities become with a bit of experience under our belts. Of course I needed to be attracted to this person as well, but for the first time ever, I considered what my Critical Personal Values were – things that were essentially not negotiable for me (commitment/marriage/children, close to their family, strong social conscience and loyalty), and I actively sought a person with these qualities.

I did this by joining an exclusive dating agency for professionals. The dating coordinator sat with me for a couple of hours and discussed the qualities of my ideal relationship in detail. We also discussed my Critical Personal Values. I was impressed with this approach.

I went on a couple of dates that were enjoyable, but nothing more than that. Carlos (who you'll meet in Chapter 5) was the third dinner date I had through the dating agency and with him I had the best conversation I had ever had with a man. I knew he was the one for me. He tells everyone I fell in love with him at first sight – which is a major exaggeration. In turn, I tease him about what he was wearing when I first met him. I could tell he'd been on his own for a while. He gave himself away by wearing his jeans just a little too high on his waist. But he was a hotty and I knew from our four-hour conversation that he had many similar Personal Values to me. This was of critical importance to me. Having my self-esteem plummet following my relationship break-up, and entering into a long and often painful road to re-build it, I was forced, agonisingly, to learn important things about myself and relationships, particularly in regards to communication and core Personal Values. My first partner was a good person. I'm a good person. And yet our relationship didn't work. I now understood that I needed to be with someone who held similar Personal Values to me about marriage and children, amongst other things.

Carlos made a second date with me before the first date ended, and I was very much looking forward to seeing him again.

**Now**

Now, watching my husband Carlos tapping away on his laptop, I'm very happy I was given a second chance at love, and this time around, I've learnt the value of meaningful two-way communications. We talk about everything, every day. I had to work hard on myself to learn appropriate communication skills. Having grown up on the cusp of the generation when children were to be seen but not heard, and then having a few critical experiences where I'd tried to speak to important people in my life about something sensitive and been yelled down or dismissed, I had learned inappropriate communication skills. Better personal communication is something I still work on to this day; our previous experiences have quite an impact on us.

When I was 38-years-old, and Carlos was 41, we started trying to fall pregnant. A year went by with no luck so we went to our doctor, who referred us straight to an IVF doctor because of our ages. There was no medical reason preventing us from falling pregnant, so we were absolutely positive that we would fall pregnant in the first round of IVF. It was a little confronting to do the injections at home, but overall, that first round was fun because we were so excited. Carlos got to see me under the effects of anaesthetic after the egg collection operation, and loved every minute of it. Apparently I'm complimentary and affectionate when I'm off my nut. He tells people it was the happiest thirty minutes of his marriage – cheeky bugger. The two-week wait to find out if we were pregnant was difficult, but we got through it and we went to the clinic on a Saturday morning for the pregnancy blood test. We had to wait until the afternoon for the call that would confirm that we were pregnant. The call came through at 2.37pm and we were devastated and shocked when the nurse said the result was negative.

It was a precursor of what was to come.

To cut a very long story short, over five years, we did over a dozen IVF cycles, including donor egg and donor embryo cycles. We had five miscarriages. We underwent adoption and foster training and assessment. All big issues, and Carlos and I didn't always automatically agree on everything we faced over that time.

Looking back at those two streamers of my life that fan out behind me, the biggest learning curve has been learning better communication skills. Not being aggressively assertive, but neither the other extreme of sweeping things under the carpet. I've found somewhere in between, where I express myself and listen in equal parts. Not only has my love relationship benefitted, so have my relationships with family and friends deepened and become more fulfilling.

Where tragedy drove my first relationship apart, challenges have strengthened Carlos and me. With each infertility setback, we were kind to each other. We talked about everything and supported each other. We made joint decisions, and we accepted the consequences of those decisions together. We've laughed, cried, sworn and fought throughout our years of trying to extend our family. Of course there are days when we annoy each other, but they're few. Some days I look at him and I can actually feel my heart hurting because I love him so much. A friend recently was talking to me about how she felt about us miscarrying our twins. She described to me seeing Carlos' face at the time and the grief and pain she saw etched into him. Her words brought tears to my eyes. When I realised that my tears were not for my lost twins, but rather from her description of seeing Carlos in pain, I realised just how deep my love for Carlos had grown. It was a profound moment for me to know that I could cry tears for Carlos even while grieving the loss of my children. Life teaches us things in unexpected ways. Ironically, less than two hours after that conversation with my friend, I returned home, full of love, to find Carlos tired, obnoxious and annoying. That's life – beautiful in its imperfections.

One of the many things I love most about my husband is that he challenges my thinking, and he says the same about me. Our personalities, previous experiences, and our problem-solving methods are different enough that we challenge each other. He's taught me much, and I've taught him much. We've widened each other's knowledge and experiences and as with all growth, it's fulfilling and empowering. I've come to believe that you know you're in the right relationship when you both are the best version of yourselves when you are together, and you both always feel safe to express your opinions and needs.

Finding myself suddenly single in my early thirties turned my world upside down. It was a long way back, but I'm so incredibly happy to be where I am right now – stronger, empowered, calmly thoughtful and in love. I believe we are meant to have a partner in this life journey, that we are stronger with the right team mate by our side.

I believe that it's worth it to put yourself out there and take another chance. You never know what amazing experiences and people might be just around the corner for you. I also believe, however, that to meet your equal, you need to do so from a position of strength. While single, I had depression and low self-esteem. Until I recovered from depression, and dealt with my low self-esteem, I didn't meet men who were right for me. It wasn't until I worked hard and largely healed, that life began falling into place.

Even though I use the phrase "life began falling into place", nothing is 'easy'. I believe that everything worthwhile takes hard work and commitment, and a good relationship is no different.

A few years ago, in Sydney, I went into a church that had lovely stained glass windows. I'm not a church goer, but I am spiritual. I went into this beautiful church surrounded by serene gardens, and with my husband beside me, I thanked God for sending me two good men to love in this lifetime. It brings me comfort to know She's looking out for me. Our forties is a great decade – I feel calm, thoughtful, grateful.

Now surrounded by my husband and kids (yes, we are now blessed with two wonderful adopted children), I couldn't be happier.

**What are your best tips for dating?**

1. Know yourself and identify in your mind what you believe makes relationships successful. Use this knowledge to have meaningful discussions with potential partners so you can see if their Personal Values gel with your own.
2. Find constructive ways to fill your days so you don't let loneliness overwhelm you. For example, I joined the Rural Fire Brigade as a volunteer and it was a challenging and fun way of spending some of my spare time. I also volunteered as the Fundraising Convenor for a charity I supported. Looking back, I should have done more things like this, and less of the drinking and partying. Live and learn. I've heard of people doing two-month treks overseas. I think physically challenging things like that are a great way of healing the soul, which is something you need to do after a break-up.
3. I like the concept of dating agencies and online dating websites. It's simply a fact that if there aren't any suitable single people in your social circle, you need to look wider to meet new people.
4. I'm a big believer in healing after a break-up, however, I know of people who are still saying ten years later that they're not yet ready to date; that they're still working out who they are. I'm not sure that there ever comes a point in time when you're 100% strong and 100% ready to date again. Meeting the right person helps finish off the healing process. When my husband proposed to me, he said these words, "You know, when we first met, we were both a little broken, but I love how strong and solid we are together. I'm excited about all the things we've already done together, and all that is to come."
5. Let the man do the chasing. Don't try to take the lead. Men chase when they're interested. If they're not interested enough to chase you,

then they aren't going to make a good long-term partner for you.

6. Don't accept last minute or late night texts as suitable date invitations. If he puts in such little effort when he's trying to impress you, what's he going to be like two years down the track when he's no longer trying to impress?
7. Be brave and put yourself out there. Unfortunately, the ideal man for you isn't going to come knocking on your door one day while you're in your jammies watching movies and eating chocolate.
8. Accept that you're normal – it lessens the loneliness. Everyone has their good days and bad days. Everyone has something in their life that they're struggling to come to terms with. Sometimes we're proud of ourselves and sometimes we're not. When you stop trying to be perfect and accept that you're simply human, a major shift happens. You relax, and everything else seems to fall into place. Love yourself; be kind to yourself. A turning point for me was reading Andre Agassi's book *Open – An Autobiography*. Here was someone I thought led a perfect life; but as it turned out, he had just as much inner turmoil as me while he matured and got to know himself. I appreciate him for openly sharing his inner thoughts and in so doing making me feel normal.
9. Don't be selfish. A relationship is not only about what you'll get out of it. It's also about what you're prepared to give another.

## Author's Notes

Jade's story gives enough detail to demonstrate how corroding it can be to individuals when Personal Values aren't aligned in a relationship. Because Jade's core value about marriage was so important to her, over time, her partner's opposite belief came to erode Jade's confidence and self-esteem. Moving forward, she describes how it was a tortuous and lengthy time to re-build those two qualities in herself.

# Key Points From Jade's Chapter

1. Effective and open communication is critically important in a relationship.
2. You know you're in the right relationship when you both are the best version of yourselves when you're together; and you both always feel safe to express your opinions and needs.
3. Have meaningful discussions with potential partners to see if their Personal Values gel with your own. Assumptions are often incorrect.

# Chapter 5

## Carlos' Story

**45-year-old Carlos admits he didn't handle his relationship break-up well, but he did get through it, and shares what happened next.**

I had a ten-year relationship that ended when I was 34-years-old. We met at university and had a lot of common ground. It was a good relationship. If I was to describe its main strength, it was based on the foundation of friendship.

My post-mortem, if I can call it that, as to why the relationship ended, is that we were at different 'places' in life, and under some very trying circumstances. I wanted children of my own. She already had one child and didn't want any more. Her career was soaring; mine was ambling. We were living away from home, in another country – England. I was missing Australia, she was settled in England.

The demise of that relationship has been the biggest tragedy I've had to overcome in my life. That's quite a large call because I've experienced some other major challenges also. We lost my family home in Latin America to an earthquake and had to live in a tent for over a year while we re-built. And when I was 20 my family and I relocated to Australia as refugees. I was half way through my university degree in

El Salvador and had to start from the beginning again when I came to Australia. That was difficult for a young man, keen to commence his career, to come to terms with. These were two challenging experiences, but my relationship break-up took far longer to overcome.

When my partner ended our relationship I was in complete denial of the truth and the reality. I didn't want to accept that I was single, and we continued living in the same house in England for 18 months following our split. I had a completely unrealistic sense of hope that everything was going to be fine. I eventually moved back home to Australia when she moved on to another relationship. Even after I moved home, I still thought we would end up back together one day. I stayed in that stage of denial and hope for three years. People tried to help me, but I refused to talk about it. I never really shared my thoughts and feelings about the break-up to my family or friends, but I have no doubt they all knew and could sense and see what I was going through.

Throughout my twenties and early thirties, I defined myself by my relationship, so when it broke down I felt I had nothing. I had to re-build myself from scratch. I was given a number of self-help books. They all helped a little. Bit by bit the 'crust' I had formed around myself was chipped away. It wasn't until possibly four years after my relationship ended that I woke up one day and said, "Enough." I can't tell you which day it was, or what finally broke through that crust, but it really took me exerting a force from within to finally break free. I started focussing on other things. I took up cycling. Getting fit made me feel good. I began to see things differently, and I slowly started looking outwardly as opposed to inwardly.

I went on a few dates. Having devoted all my energy to my work over the last four years, my career was doing well and my work sponsored me to go to an overseas conference. I took the opportunity to stop in England and visit my former partner and step-daughter. Sharon wasn't doing very well at that time. Her relationship had broken down, and I was still hung up on her, so that visit fuelled my hope again.

Sharon never actually told me that there was no hope for us. But when she got another boyfriend after her break-up, I finally realised that we weren't going to get back together. To be fair, looking back, she may have been 100% clear that we wouldn't get back together, but I just didn't want to hear it.

I was in a lot of pain for a very long time. You could argue that it was self-inflicted pain and I just didn't want to get out of that rut. Healing was a slow process. I don't recommend what I did, and if I had my time again I would do things differently. Looking back, I do understand why it was the way it was. I wish I'd had more friends at the time – good friends who could have helped me get out of the rut I was in. During my relationship with Sharon, we were very self-reliant and felt we didn't need anyone, so I became isolated from friends. Also, my traditional Catholic parents didn't approve of her – a single mother – so it was easier for me to isolate myself from everyone. So when the relationship ended, I had no-one around me to rely on. Sometimes, as an individual, we're not 100% equipped to deal with the sad reality. I was hearing what I wanted to hear – that there was hope for us to get back together, instead of what Sharon was actually telling me. We can be our own worst counsellors. We're all mature and fairly self-reliant, but when it comes to crises we don't always have the right answers for ourselves. We need someone who can give an unbiased view. If I had of had more friends around me at the time, and if I had of been more open about what was happening to me, I might have received and heard that advice. But that wasn't the case.

At the time, I could not, in all good conscience, commit myself to someone else without first being rid of all that past and pain. It wasn't a case of cutting Sharon and my step-daughter Jaimee out of my life – I'm still friends with Sharon, and Jaimee has a special place in my heart – you can't simply switch off that kind of paternal love. However, I needed to be human again, to be able to honestly and genuinely say, "Yes, I'm through, I'm free, I can commit to another person."

When I felt I reached that point, I started to interact more consciously with other people. I got myself out there, way out of my comfort zone. I vividly remember chatting to a mate and he was saying he wanted to do something different, and he wanted to take Latin dance lessons. Most Hispanics are natural dancers. I'm not. I figured I could do with some lessons so thought, "Why not?" and went along with him. Other work colleagues joined us and it became quite a tight knit group. My mate met his wife there. I also got involved in team sports – beach volleyball and mixed netball. I worked for a large company and became a lot more involved in the work social scene. Work sponsored me for another conference in Budapest, and I still took a side trip to see Sharon and Jaimee. Even then, I still had feelings for Sharon, but that visit was the final goodbye for me. My feelings were on the way out – thank God!

After that trip, I genuinely started noticing girls more. I went on a few dates. They seemed to start well, but after a few dates I usually wasn't 'feeling it'. I fell for one girl at work, only to find that she decided to start dating someone else. That was a bit of a blow – she was the first girl I'd liked since Sharon.

I met another girl and at first we hit it off. We even watched the World Cup Soccer together. She then went away on a holiday, and when she returned she was quite hostile towards me. I didn't understand and it knocked my confidence.

I also met an Hispanic girl while cycling. She was older than me, and spoke fluent Spanish. We enjoyed that connection, but early on it became apparent that I wanted children and she didn't so the relationship petered away before it started.

That, coupled with the other dating experiences that went nowhere, said to me that I wasn't meeting the right people. I don't believe in continuing to do the same thing, and expecting a different answer.

I decided to take the initiative in quite an unconventional way for a good Catholic lad. I contacted a couple of dating agencies, but when I spoke with them I didn't have a good feeling about them. For instance, one was saying they would give me a contract to sign, but then got upset at me when I wanted to read the contract before signing it! I decided to try one more, and the lady met me at a coffee shop and we spoke for a couple of hours. She asked me a lot of questions. She really established who I was, what I was about, what my Personal Values were, and what I was looking for in a relationship. I liked that she spent so much time with me and felt encouraged that if she was doing the same with the women she interviewed that she would be able to recommend like-minded people for introductions.

I was quietly terrified, somewhat encouraged, and also a little bit embarrassed to be resorting to a dating agency. I was feeling inadequate at not being able to meet anyone on my own.

Katie, the lady from the dating agency, sent me two profiles. I had coffee with both ladies but didn't go on a second date with either. Then Katie contacted me and said she had two new profiles for me. One of them was a writer, which I found intriguing. I liked the look of her photo, and she had a really lovely smile. Her name was Jade.

I was nervous, but this was my third time on a blind date so I had some experience under my belt. I remember Jade called me to ask if I was there. She wanted to know where I was sitting. I thought it was good that she was confident and happy enough to call me like that. I can still totally picture the moment I first saw her. She was wearing a black ensemble – a fitted dress shirt with pants and strappy heels. She was stunning. I loved her long blonde hair, and I really liked what she was wearing.

We had a lovely time. I felt comfortable right from the start. We engaged; there was a connection there. We talked for hours. The date went from strength to strength and we went from a cuppa to dinner. At the end we both said we'd like to see each other again.

I was nervous the first time I called her after that initial meeting, but I shouldn't have been. We organised to meet again. We went on subsequent dates with increasing levels of affection over time, and the rest is history.

With Jade it was exciting, scary, easy, nice. Nothing was laboured. Nothing was difficult. There was nothing fake about Jade, or our time together. She was easy going, unlike anyone I had ever met before in my life. I thought she was beautiful. I can't tell you if I fell in love with her on that first encounter, but maybe I did. What I do know is that she shattered that crust I had formed around myself. I could see myself taking things forward with her, and with that came a realisation that I was moving on to a new chapter in my life, and hopefully a better chapter.

We had a short honeymoon period – as in that mesmerising, starry-eyed period – because we weren't young. We were mid-thirties, and it became clear that we both came from similar backgrounds in a romantic sense. We had both had long-term relationships and we were both hurt by, and unprepared for, their demise. We were both certain about what we did and didn't want in our next relationship. There was no bullshit. We were both financially secure and lived in our own homes. We lived an hour apart so remaining connected and seeing each other during the week required work. But it was never a chore. Seeing her was always a delight. We would meet for dinner, have a kiss. We would try to maximise the time we spent together on the weekends.

Whilst we had similar Personal Values, we were also very different people. We got to show each other completely new worlds. We both had a lot of heritage to share. For instance, she took me out to my first stand-up comedy experience at the Powerhouse Theatre in Brisbane. That night is one of my best memories. I introduced her to my family, to my way of life, and bike riding. I met and liked her friends. She met and liked mine. My friends took to her.

One defining and liberating experience for me was taking Jade to my work Christmas party. I had worked there for years, but had purposely avoided the Christmas parties because I was still grieving and didn't feel like partying at all. The year before I did attend on my own and had a great time, and then the following year I showed up with Jade without having told anyone I had a girlfriend. I shocked them all. They were intrigued by this creative, intelligent, blonde bombshell.

I enjoyed having a girlfriend.

Things were going well so I invited her on a 5-week overseas holiday to Russia and Eastern Europe with me, my parents and my brother. That was our first challenge. Jade struggled a little with the close-knit nature of my family. My Father, Mother, brother and I can easily spend 24 hours a day for weeks on end together. Jade's family is close, but they're all very independent from each other.

When we returned I got offered a significant promotion but it required moving interstate. At that time, Jade and I had been dating for a year, and we were still living an hour away from each other. I didn't want things to end, so I asked if she would come with me. At first she said we should commute for a while and see how our relationship panned out, but a few weeks before I was due to leave, she changed her mind and said she was prepared to join me. I was over the moon about that.

We moved cities, and moved in together, at the same time. There we were – two mature people combining two households and one cat. They say that in terms of stress, moving house is third only to death and divorce. What the hell were we thinking – moving interstate and in together for the first time, at the same time? It was certainly interesting for a while. But it was worth it. We have now married and have a solid, happy marriage. She makes me smile every day.

**What have you learned about relationships?**

They will surprise you. Expect the unexpected. Never take anything for granted. They are ever changing. They will frustrate you, anger you at times, make you cry, but … they will also provide you with all the happiness you ever imagined. They will fulfil, challenge and reward you. It's possibly the single most worthwhile endeavour that you can embark on. It's not all about yourself. It's about yourself in the context of being with another human being. Relationships teach you humility and resilience.

**How does your second relationship differ from your first?**

I think my second relationship is what you would call a more mature love – more measured and conscious. No less passionate though. My first relationship was formative. Don't get me wrong, I treasure my first relationship even though it ended. I'm glad it happened because it gave me so much. The single biggest gift I guess is my step-daughter, Jaimee. But it also gave me a friend – Sharon.

My second relationship has given me everything. It's a bit of a cliché – you hear these phrases in movies – but they tend to be true. She completes me. Our relationship has given me humility and perspective. It has challenged me, and rewarded me incredibly. If I was to compare, in every time that I have been challenged at work, stepping up to meet those challenges has rewarded me incredibly. My second relationship is the same – it has been challenging and foreign but hugely rewarding. She is my equal, she is my better. She is everything I'm not and more. We are alike and dissimilar at the same time. I can only imagine how she's going to age. She's going to be like a fine wine because each year she gets even better with age.

Jade and I are now blessed with a son and a daughter. I'm thrilled for our kids that they can experience of Jade what I get to experience. She's a wonderful person and an incredible mother. She's still growing every day too. It's hard to fathom all that she's capable of.

Part of being with another person can be incredibly frustrating, and at other times, simply amazing. There's nowhere else I would rather be, and no-one else I would rather be with. There's a saying I like – home is where someone runs to greet you.

**What advice would you give to a mate who was stuck in a rut after a relationship break-up?**

If you ever find yourself in a crap position – and we all do at some point in our lives – be aware that it is possible to get out of that position, and get in a better one. The decision lies within you.

It shouldn't have taken me four years to move past my break-up, but at the time I chose to stay that way.

Having a good relationship with another human being is within one's choice and one's grasp, and it is worth giving it a go.

I was good enough on my own – I discovered that. I got to the point where I knew I was going to be okay on my own. But I'm that much better being part of a duo, than being a solo act.

**What do you think are the biggest mistakes people make in relationships?**

Taking the other person for granted, and being numb in certain situations. In my case, I became unaware of my other half. Successful relationships are about meeting needs. So long as each party is having their needs met, the relationship will succeed. Quite often we focus on our own needs and become oblivious to our partner's needs, and that is a recipe for disaster. It has to be a two-way street.

**What are your suggestions for healing after a relationship break-up?**

Each person is different. In my particular situation I think I needed to grieve and I allowed myself that period of grieving. Seek counsel, and listen to it. Depending on how early or late a person is in the grieving process, the advice will have a different effect, but it will have an effect. Allow it to do so. Listen. One good action I took was to read books that shared experiences and gave me different perspectives. I even kept some photocopies of things I thought were good, practical advice. Try new things. Dance … anything to get out of the rut. Change your environment. If a person's life is a picture – take a new picture. I find physical activity quite therapeutic so I took on bike riding and that was a great action for me. It gave me routine, purpose and a social life.

## Author's Notes

It's interesting how many of the interviewees found exercise to be their therapy. Getting fit made Carlos feel good which cascaded into thinking about things differently.

Carlos gave some good advice in terms of grief following a relationship breakup. With hindsight, Carlos was able to identify that his grief most likely took longer to evolve because he shut himself off from those around him. Talking to trusted friends or a professional will help you process your grief.

# Key Points From Carlos' Chapter

1. When it comes to crises we don't always have the right answers for ourselves. Sometimes we need someone who can give an unbiased view.
2. Having a good relationship with another human being is within one's choice and one's grasp, and it's worth giving it a go.
3. Take a new picture – carve a happier future.

# Chapter 6

### Elena's Story

**Six years ago, Singer and Florist, Elena, thought she would never be able to love again when her partner ran off with her best friend's daughter. The pain and betrayal nearly overwhelmed her.**

My first marriage lasted 19 years, but ultimately disintegrated because the man I married had developed alcoholism and schizophrenia. We produced three beautiful and talented children. My husband was a footballer and embroiled in the big drinking culture that came with it. I've often wondered if it was the heavy drinking that brought on the mental illness.

After seven years on my own, I met my second partner and for fourteen years I thought I was happy, until he ran off with my best friend's daughter, a woman twenty years my junior.

My best friend, her daughter and I sang together as a trio harmony group and my partner was our roadie/soundman. I cooked dinner for my friend and her daughter every Wednesday night while we practised. I actually served that girl food in my home!

The sense of betrayal was unbelievably painful. I was 60-years-old, without a home, broken hearted and full of fear. I lost my partner, my best friend, and my singing trio all in one fell swoop. At the time, those three things were such a large part of my life.

Have you ever noticed that people who have affairs think they're not going to get caught, and yet they always do? I found out about my partner's affair because a lady, who was a bit of a gossip and worked at one of the clubs where we sang, told me that "people" had suspicions and I should find out what was going on. The temperature from my body was like a furnace moving up me. I went and sat, watching my partner setting up on stage, mulling over the gossip's words. I realised that in recent times I would often turn around and both my partner and our third singer would be gone. I felt hollow, empty and puzzled. We were at an outdoor festival and I decided I had to find out for sure.

I went looking for her. She was sitting in a pub with her partner and daughter. She offered me a drink and we walked to the bar together. Alone with her, I said, "I want to know from you, is it true?"

She replied, "I don't want to talk about it."

With that reply, I knew it was true. I chose not to make a scene in front of her family. I got up and left. It was time to confront my partner. He was still setting up on stage and there were hundreds of people around. I was sitting there on the grass, hiding I guess, feeling heat and trauma in my body. I felt like my body was breaking down. I guess it's your glands doing their fight or flight thing – it felt like poison moving through my entire body. When he finished, we went by the water to eat some pizza. I confronted him. He responded angrily, saying, "You think everyone should think like you." I watched him walk away and I fed the pelicans my pizza.

That night I stayed with my daughter, and the next day when I returned to our unit, most of his things were gone. There was a note and money on the table. The note said, "Left money for two weeks rent. I might be back in three weeks to get the rest of my stuff." That is how significant the note was after fourteen years with him! I changed the locks.

After three weeks he returned to get his belongings. He gave me a cuddle and couldn't stop crying, saying, "I'm so sorry, I've done the most awful thing." I cried too, but I didn't want him back by then. However, I was secretly hoping that he wanted me back so I could reject him. It didn't happen that way. He looked at all his stuff and asked if I could arrange to get it to a local charity. He asked if I would go buy a sandwich for lunch. He handed me $5 and when I returned he asked for his change back! I shouldn't have been surprised, he always was mean with money.

When we said our farewells I was calm and precise, saying to him, "Both of you are like Judas was to Jesus; you have both betrayed me."

Seeing him gave me resolve to be strong. Not only was he stingy about the sandwich money, there was no offer of help from him to transport all his things to the charity. He just wanted to leave and get back to his new life. I didn't feel anything when he left that day. They had poisoned me with their betrayal.

For months I felt ill and couldn't eat much. I spent every night at my daughter's house. I didn't want to live in 'our' unit anymore, but actually moving my whole life and finances by myself was overwhelming so for a while I did nothing about it. Eventually my daughter and I packed everything up and I moved into her place. It was hard. I kept myself busy, but no matter what I did I felt like I was outside everything; like a non-entity. People say that Sunday night is the hardest night for single people. I found that every night when I knocked off work I felt lost. It was cruel.

My daughter asked me what I wanted for my life and I couldn't answer her. I worked two jobs and went through the motions of day-to-day life to get through. I was very busy and lost 9kgs. It was a significant amount off my small frame.

I did a lot of self-reflection. I belonged to the Uniting Church – they were my spiritual family. I was part of a group called Care and Share, a church group for women to support each other. There were older women and a few my age, women I had connected with for many years. In a small town you have a connection to friends and it's a deep and meaningful one. They gave me lots of material to read and it felt like every time I turned the page there was something significant for me in the scripture readings. And then my Mum passed away and while my family and I were packing up her stuff, I came across Mum's Bible. It had her writing all the way through it. My brothers and sister didn't want it. I felt like it was meant for me. When I went back to my other reading material and it would say, "Read verse such and such", I would go to Mum's Bible and there would be her handwriting. I felt like she was talking to me. Life is all about timing.

I found being single to be very difficult for the first 12 months. I cried a lot, often sobbing in the shower. At work, people probably got sick of my need to talk and question over and over again … "Why? Why did it happen? What did I do wrong? Why was I not good enough?" I try to have empathy for people in this situation now and to be patient with them because I understand what they're going through. One of the 30-year-old guys at work was laid back about my need to talk about it, so I peppered him with my questions about men.

I heard that dear friends of mine put my ex and his mistress up in their house when they came to town to visit. That broke my heart. I felt betrayed.

My daughter and son-in-law were wonderful. They had me at their house for three months. But after that it was time for me to move on and release my daughter from the responsibility of looking after me. With my brothers' and sister's blessing, I moved into our Mum's house. Mum's house has a wonderful view of the mountains and lake. The calm engulfed me. I could feel Mum's and Dad's presence there; warm and caring. I was lonely, but healing. The blessings came in little things like butterflies flying into the room, or random people dropping in for companionship. The neighbours were friendly and there were always children playing and screaming in the street after 3pm, and then around 6pm their Mums would yell out and call them inside and the street would go quiet again. I loved all the noise and routine. I was coming back into the real world.

This is a letter I wrote to myself during my healing. I needed to keep telling myself these things until I actually believed them.

*3rd May, 2007*

*Dearest Elena,*

*I am writing to you because I have heard about your sadness and pain. You are a most beautiful person with a heart of gold.*

*I'm so sorry that you have endured such heartache and pain over the last 13 weeks. To be treated so disrespectfully was nearly more than you could endure. But by the grace of God and the Universe Angels and the positive love of your beautiful daughter, son-in-law, and true friends, you are flying through this time on the wings of an eagle.*

*You did not deserve any of what was dealt you, but it had to come did it not? You knew life was on eggshells and the angst of his personality was such you kept taking it on and on. Now you know – find your authentic self.*

*The music and travel of that time was wonderful and I know you learnt much through all that. Singing in the trio was a magic time and the experience can't be replaced, but it all came at a cost to you. Know that only positive things can come out of this journey as the will of your thoughts and feelings will speed you on into new realms of new dreams and loves. It's only a matter of time. Don't give up or give in to the low times. The blessings of your daughter and your beautiful friends are so uplifting that you will never be alone. Your Mum is always with you. What wonderful role models you've had.*

*The pain came and the pain will dissipate sooner than you can imagine. You had to go through this to come out the other side. There is someone special for you. The Universe and God know who it is but you will see this in near time. You'll know that someone can and will love you for the beautiful person you are.*

*You're in the 'light' and being looked after by the Universe and your positive thoughts. You are flying high – the pain is almost gone. Just keep strong in mind and body and be proud of who you are.*

*Love You Always*

*Elena*
*xxxx*

Around this time I was drawn to a group called *The Spiritual Circle*. Every month they would have a different guest speaker. It was all about angels, fairies, crystals, and the like. One guest speaker talked about breathing out the negatives and taking in positive energy. When you're at these groups, everyone is there for a specific purpose individual to them. It's about sharing. It was like an awakening for me. Another speaker touched on Sleep Clearing. This immediately helped me. As part of my grief over my relationship loss, sleep had become scarce. He taught me to recite positive statements about my day, my future and my past. I did this every night. It was a wonderful process to regain the benefits of self-love.

I was searching for answers as to why I was dumped for a younger woman. In the end, I found the answer for me – that every relationship has a timing in my life. We go through life to learn and some people come into our life only for a period of time to teach us something. Learning is an honourable thing.

I was yearning for another partner the whole time I was going through my period of self-reflection and healing. I don't necessarily believe that you need to be on your own until you feel happy on your own. I'm a character who needs people. I was the second eldest of eight siblings and I was used to having people around me. Whilst I wasn't totally comfortable in my own skin, I still had a lot to offer someone. I have a friend who has been on her own for years because she doesn't think she's ready to be in a relationship yet. I would love to show her what opens up when you share your heart. Sometimes, taking a chance and allowing someone new into your heart completes the healing process.

Some single women in my life started talking about online dating. They were meeting people, but I wasn't comfortable with the idea. Instead I joined a Christian singles group and was introduced to a man who I went on a few dates with. He got drunk and fell over in my garden and all the experiences from my first marriage came flooding back. I never saw him again.

The singles market in country towns is lean. My friends convinced me to put my profile on an internet dating site. Oh, that is an hilarious thing to do. The way you talk about yourself on your profile, well, let me just say, it isn't natural to talk about yourself like that! I changed my profile many times before I was happy with it. Online dating wasn't an addiction for me. I didn't have much time to go on it. I didn't answer many people who contacted me. For instance, if they didn't have a photo on their profile I simply deleted them.

One of my girlfriends asked me to go on a holiday with her. I had long service leave, so we went on a 10-week caravanning adventure. We were like Thelma and Louise, doing everything ourselves. We could back the van, grease the ball and chain, and check the caravan battery. Our personalities balanced each other well; we never fought. As we drove along for hours and hours, we cried and laughed and talked. It was cleansing.

We felt we were in paradise most of the time. We met many backpackers along the way. We met a backpacking songwriter who asked us to go to the CWA Hall to help teach some people his song. The next day, we stopped at the one coffee shop in the little town and there he was again. We had a great chat about music and life and then we never saw him again. These are the types of random adventures you have when you're travelling. We took a tour out into the bush to birthing caves of the indigenous people. It was a lovely, eye-opening time. It's amazing that when you open yourself up to experiences, special people, relevant to where you're at, at the time, come into your life; sometimes only for fleeting but meaningful encounters. We had an amazing experience watching a concert at a sugar cane plantation. We had dinner and then moved to timber seats in an outdoor amphitheatre in the cane fields. It was a full moon that night and there was a violinist, piano player and a singer. It was an incredibly moving experience.

I was already quite strong before I went, but this holiday made me even stronger. Healing the past happened along the way during that entire holiday, and at the same time the future was starting to lead me to a better place … through texts and conversations during the trip with a man I met online.

Sydney contacted me on the online dating site just before my friend and I left on our caravanning holiday. When I saw his photo I thought he had a lovely face and decided to answer him. We didn't have a chance to meet before my holiday, but he kept in contact while I was away. I think it was good for us that we got to know each other for so long before we met in person. Small amounts of information each time, in a text or short call, gradually built up. I left on my holiday with a terrible flu and short, dark hair. I came home tanned, relaxed and with longer hair streaked with blonde. I was feeling sensational within myself; emotionally strong and carefree.

The first time I met Sydney in person was on a Saturday in the foyer of the RSL Club where I worked. I felt safe there surrounded by people I knew. I wasn't too nervous, just excited, and I immediately felt relaxed in his company. The connection was nice and easy. On our first date we had a cup of tea and a sandwich and discovered we were into the same sorts of things; eg. bike riding, canoeing, travel, swimming. He gave me a quick kiss when he left and did a little happy dance shimmy. I liked that!

I'd started rock-n-roll dancing, and Sydney was already in a rock-n-roll group. We went out dancing with friends one night, and when he dropped me home I felt butterflies. It was a nice feeling. I had thought that I would never experience that again. From then on, I walked around with a smile on my face.

It took me three relationships, but this time around, I've found the right person for me. There's a book called *In The Meantime*. It talks about the journey of learning in life. It showed me how to learn from repeated patterns and how I previously accepted less than my self-worth. I grew up in an age when women were raised to give and not think about what we wanted for ourselves. I had come full circle now, and finally, I knew myself well enough to listen to my instinct, and my instincts about Sydney were all good.

In one of my self-reflective moments I had written this list of qualities that I wanted in my next relationship:

1. To give and receive love, caring, self-love, own acceptance.
2. Harmony, peace, sharing, cooperation.
3. Faithfulness and trust.
4. Reverence for life, laughter, adventure, happiness.
5. Humbleness.
6. Courage.
7. Commitment, respectfulness, kindness, compassion, forgiveness.
8. Affectionate and sexual.
9. Love of the Lord.
10. Willing to share our finances as a team.
11. Good communicator.
12. Slim body, good health, good teeth, taller than me.
13. Night owl, doesn't snore.

Sydney is most of these things. Sydney and I call ourselves a work-in-progress. We each have so much personal history that there is a bit of push and pull, but mostly there is love, sharing, caring and adventure. We're a great match.

I was raised in a generation where a woman's sole purpose was to look after their house and their family. Also, my generation grew up affected by the Vietnam War. We lost parents, brothers and sisters, and we married men who had Post-traumatic Stress Disorder. We didn't think of our own needs, other than wanting a house to live in.

It's interesting to consider the hierarchy of needs I had at each intersection of my life.

**Hierarchy of Needs for my First Marriage**

1. Marriage.
2. House.
3. Children.
4. Friendship.
5. Church.

**Hierarchy of Needs for my Second Relationship**

1. To be loved.
2. Marriage.
3. House.
4. Emotional support and connection with my partner.

**Hierarchy of Needs for my Current Relationship**

1. Love, affection, caring, emotional support.
2. Great sexual intimacy and connection with a giving partner.
3. Negotiation and harmony in the relationship.
4. Trust.
5. Sharing our finances as a team.

6. Courage.
7. Laughter and joy.
8. Respect, including respect and inclusion for my children.
9. Common interests.
10. Similar taste in music.
11. Similar religious beliefs.
12. Commitment.
13. Humility.
14. Adventure.
15. Non-judgemental.
16. Willing to change and grow as we learn together.

My generation, particularly the women, weren't taught to think of 'self'. It's taken me many years to un-learn this. There's no way that I will ever settle for co-existing again. One of the most important things I have learned throughout my three relationships has been healing. My life outside my relationships has always been joyful with singing, music, performing and adventure being a huge part of my life. Now I have learned to have a joyful love relationship as well.

I have to admit though, I do still struggle sometimes with totally being myself. One of the biggest hurdles coming into a new relationship later in life is getting used to each other's little idiosyncrasies. I still have trouble sometimes with the tone of voice I use on Sydney. I think it's the mother's voice in me. The words you use, tone, look; how you come across to each other is a big thing. Sydney will sometimes be offended by my words and tone so I try to adjust my language style.

I've learnt that what works in one relationship, may not work in another. You have to be prepared to change. For instance, a joke that may have been funny in one relationship, might be offensive in another. Different sleeping patterns can also be a big hurdle to overcome.

As a couple you have to learn new accepted norms that are right for your current relationship. Sydney and I are both happy to change to accommodate each other, and open to trying to understand each other. I think that's very important. You grow and learn together every day.

**What do you think are the common mistakes that people make in relationships?**

1. Listening too much to the emotional endorphins and letting those cloud our judgement.
2. Lack of commitment and thinking the grass is greener on the other side. It generally isn't – all relationships require effort and maintenance.
3. Not knowing our authentic self, not knowing what our Personal Values are, and being unable to reasonably express them.
4. Being too selfish about our own needs.
5. Resisting change and growth.
6. Being too intolerant.

**What do you think makes a great relationship?**

1. Sharing.
2. Honest and open communication with negotiation and positive speaking.
3. Being positive and happy – treat your partner as you wish to be treated.
4. Belief in a higher power.
5. Sexual intimacy.
6. Family getting on and accepting each other.
7. Similar Personal Values.

# Author's Notes

Sixty-years-old and thrown away for a woman 20 years her junior! One could forgive Elena for wallowing in self-pity. And she did for a while. But then she picked herself up and moved on. I'm fairly certain you admire her strength and spunk just as much as I do. Now it's time for you to be someone others admire. Find your strength, and let it shine. It's okay if you need time to grieve, but be reasonable, don't let yourself stay stuck there. You're an intelligent human being, you know if you've been grieving too long. If you have, change it. If you're grieving in a healthy way, allow yourself the time, and then move on, and upwards. Elena chose travel, natural healing therapies and spirituality. What's your path to healing?

# Key Points From Elena's Chapter

1. Don't move too quickly into a new relationship, but also don't resist change when it's time. Sometimes, taking a chance and allowing someone new into your heart completes the healing process.
2. When you open yourself up to experiences, special people, relevant to where you're at, come into your life.
3. When entering into a new relationship, as a couple you learn new accepted norms. You grow and learn together every day, however, for this process to be positive, your Personal Values must align. To know if your Personal Values align with a new prospective partner, you need to know what your critical Personal Values are – those you are willing to negotiate on, and those that are non-negotiable.

# Chapter 7

## Sydney's Story

**Sydney is Elena's partner. This fit, youthful 70-year-old has a calm, down-to-earth, succinct approach. He found love via internet dating.**

When you get out there and talk to people it's amazing the doors that open up for you.

I was 67-years-old when I put my profile on an internet dating site. Some people asked me if it was confronting, but no, I simply thought I'd give it a go. I looked on it as a fairly straight-forward process.

I would caution people considering putting themselves online to be truthful on their profile. If you click with someone, you are going to meet them face-to-face eventually so why try to be disingenuous? I'm very active – bike riding, walking, rock-n-roll dancing, canoeing. I'm lean and fit and I was looking for someone with similar interests as myself because I wanted to share this lifestyle with my partner. One particular lady who I met up with for a coffee wrote "slim" on her profile and had her headshot cropped fairly tightly. When I met her, she was overweight. I didn't ask why she did that, but I'm assuming that because she had such a lovely personality she thought that people would overlook the weight when they met her. It doesn't work that way. When you're searching for a partner you're looking for someone with compatible interests to yourself. If someone lies on their profile that makes this difficult. Lying includes not using a current photo.

Having said all that, I would encourage anyone my age with the desire to give online dating a try to go ahead. It's a great way to access the singles pool. It's hard meeting people at clubs. Through online dating you get to email them for some time before you decide if you want to meet them in person. Blokes seem to have it a lot easier to be honest. On the internet dating site and at rock-n-roll dances I went to, there were always far more single ladies than there were men. Maybe it's true that women outlive men! Or maybe the blokes are sitting at home, not doing anything.

I've had two previous marriages and both of them lasted for around twenty years. I'm not used to living by myself; I need companionship. When I'm by myself I keep busy with running and cycling and spending time with my brother and sister and my grown-up kids. I have a great time doing all that, but then on Sunday night I would come home to an empty house, and I simply didn't like it.

While I was single, I had some single mates, but they just liked sitting around the clubs and drinking. I prefer to be outside doing physical exercise. You're never too old to start a fitness program. Keeping fit gives you motivation to do so much more with your life. I'm 70 and I walk my dog, Toby, twice a day, do a 20km bike ride 4-5 times a week, and on the weekend do a 40km ride. I think physical activity is a great way to meet people. There are always clubs and groups to join, and advertisements in the paper for walking groups, etc.

When I decided to put myself out there and try online dating, I didn't tell my kids at first. When they did find out they were very supportive. I didn't go on too many dates. I would meet a lady for coffee and if there wasn't any chemistry I wouldn't take it any further. I did invite two ladies out to dinner, but those didn't progress past the second date.

After meeting a lady online, I didn't stress too much about my answers in my emails to her. I wasn't nervous or apprehensive at all. To me, it was simply a great way to meet people; I was never emotionally invested at that stage of the process.

When I met Elena it felt right from the start. Just after I met her online, she went away on an extended holiday with a girlfriend of hers, so we had a long time getting to know each other over email before we met in person. The first time we did meet up, we had a nice lunch. She was active and learning rock-n-roll dancing. The following week I met up with her again and she brought a friend along. I liked her friend, which I thought was another good sign. We all went to a dance together. I had a smile on my face after that dance. I was definitely keen on her. We went out for another meal and another night of dancing and it was still all good. Things kicked on smoothly from there. There were no hiccups along the way; we simply got on really well.

Despite that, there was a bit of an adjustment period when we first moved in together. Elena is a night owl, whereas I like to get up at 5.30am to go bike riding. There was no yelling or anything, but we certainly had to negotiate with each other to find "our" way. We both compromised a bit and now go to bed about 10pm. It can be unsettling to have to change long-standing habits.

I think in relationships you have to do that – both compromise and meet each other half way. I know people who are set in their ways and expect their partner to do things their way. I find those people, and by that I mean selfish people, usually don't have many friends. Everybody has got to be a bit flexible in a relationship to make it work.

People can definitely learn to negotiate. It's something that probably comes with experience in relationships. I've found that it's important to sit down and talk openly and honestly about how each other feels and how our individual choices impact on each of us. You have to negotiate without being too emotional. It can be difficult to negotiate when one partner gets withdrawn. I would sooner talk it out, rather than close off and say nothing. I think anyone who has been in a relationship where there has been a lot of animosity will agree that in the long run, it's just not worth it. If it's that toxic that you can't get on together, and can't negotiate with each other, then really, there's no point.

Living together is certainly more challenging than dating. Communication becomes even more vital once you move in together. I also think it's important to set goals together. Elena and I want to go to New Zealand for a holiday soon, and we're about to buy a kayak. We live near a lake so we want to take advantage of that.

I felt comfortable with Elena right from the start. I feel happy, comfortable and content now. I wake up every day with a smile on my face. She doesn't hog the bed.

**What have you learnt about relationships?**

1. There's a lot of give and take and you have to be flexible about the way you think.
2. It's a work-in-progress.
3. Never go to bed cranky. Always work it out first.
4. A similar sense of humour goes a long way.

**What are your top tips for meeting women?**

1. Rock-n-roll dancing.
2. Online dating.
3. Physical activity groups, such as walking groups.
4. Volunteering. All activity that gets you out of the house and meeting people when you're single will open up your network to new opportunities and new people. You just never know where that one person who is right for you will be waiting.

# Author's Notes

Interestingly, we're already seeing some consistent themes on tackling singlehood. Physical exercise and opening yourself up to new experiences rated highly across all age groups I interviewed.

Obviously, internet dating worked for Sydney and Elena. If you want to give online dating a go, here are some tips to protect yourself and maximise the opportunity. Online dating is a tool that has helped many people find love.

1. Use a current photo.
2. Be absolutely honest about yourself in your profile.
3. Don't use provocative user names; eg. EasyGirl or OnTheRebound are unlikely to attract serious contenders for the title of your next committed partner.
4. Be patient.
5. Enter into communications with people whose profiles convey similar interests and Personal Values as your own.
6. Discover more about your mutual interests and Personal Values by using email and phone for some time before meeting in person.
7. When you do meet in person, do so in a public place.
8. Take things slowly. It takes time to get to know people, and this is particularly important when you're getting to know a stranger that you've met online. You don't have the benefit of a personal introduction with known history. Think about giving your connection the time and space a traditional friendship would have to form. Give your friendship time to grow before taking things to an intimate level. This helps weed out the people who are only looking for a fling.
9. Trust your intuition.

# Key Points From Sydney's Chapter

1. If you're going to try online dating, be truthful on your profile, including using a current photo.
2. You're never too old to start a fitness program, and it's a great way of meeting people.
3. Get out there. You just never know where that one person who is right for you will be.

# Chapter 8

## Caroline's Story

**31-years-old and single, Caroline is a Geologist. She's comfortable being single. Career, a solid friendship base, active social life, and a well-stocked wine cupboard see her in a happy place. She's open to love when it happens; not feeling an urgency to seek it out as a priority. She makes some interesting observations about dating.**

I've had two major love relationships. The first, when I was 17-years-old, was full of teen angst, incredibly passionate, up and down, with awesome highs. My Dad once said that this relationship sucked the colour out of me. I went from wearing bright colours to brown, baggy cords. It was a stressful relationship because when it was great it was brilliant, but when it was bad, it was very bad.

I'm attracted to creative souls because I find they're passionate about life. They can also be tortured individuals though. To be fair, so can I.

My second relationship started when I was 22, and ended when I was 26. This relationship shaped me. He did a lot of 'fixing' me in terms of enabling me to be emotionally intimate. We shared a common interest in rock metal and punk grunge. He was a good guy, but he wasn't grown up. A lot of the things I loved about him also ultimately drove us apart. I loved his creative streak, but practical day-to-day stuff was a nightmare. We talked of marriage and kids in the beginning. He was the one who brought it up and together we dreamt of a wedding in a castle. He was going to wear a kilt and I was going to have a deep red, corseted dress.

However, we weren't intellectual equals and he wasn't comfortable that I earned more than him. We broke up three times. During our second break-up, I explored overseas work opportunities. When those opportunities later became a reality, it sealed the beginning of the end. I did a stint working in Russia and by that time I was wanting more out of life, and less out of him.

The world is a big place and there are lots of things to do; it has to be a very special person to stop me from wanting to pack a suitcase.

I've now been single for six years. I'm meeting men, just not the right one yet. As you get older it becomes more difficult to meet them. In our twenties there is certainly a bigger circle of single people around us. Now I work in an office and see a defined number of people and see them regularly – it couldn't be more different to university life. The 'potentials' I meet tend to have some connection to work and as the saying goes, you have to be careful about crapping where you eat.

I don't have any trouble meeting single men. I categorise them into two groups – 'potentials' and 'randoms' – potential relationship material, and randoms who might be fun for short flings. You can meet randoms anywhere. Potentials are rare.

I signed up to an online dating website and had a bit of a revelation. If you don't put in serious effort, you won't get results. I've come to view it like a work proposal to bid on a new job. You aren't going to win if you don't put your best effort into the document. I only put in a half-hearted effort. It's good that online dating sites exist, but they aren't for me. I prefer to get involved in things around me, and if I meet someone, and I like them, then it's nice to go out on a few dates and explore the connection.

I'm comfortable going out with friends or on my own. I've been to music festivals on my own. When I'm watching a band I love, I almost always meet other people who share my love of that band. I also sometimes go to the theatre on my own. At interval, I'll be there with my wine browsing the programs and guys will come up and start chatting. In a way, it's easier for men to approach you when you're alone. At the pub with friends I get absorbed in conversations. We are a tight group, mostly couples. It would be quite intimidating for anyone to come up and make a move in that environment.

**What type of man are you looking for?**

My most fulfilling times have always been spent with artists, so most likely I will end up with a creative man. He has to be passionate about things, and have an independent life; ie. be fulfilled within himself. There are always adjustments to allow someone to fit in with your life, but he has to have a life outside of me. If I could find someone stronger than me in a verbal smack down, that would be awesome. I do have a tendency to dominate.

**What turns you off when dating?**

There is something off-putting about meeting someone who knows they want a relationship. I find it odd that some people want to be married so badly that it doesn't seem to matter to whom. Some people can be way too intense on the first few dates. Admittedly, it's hard to be relaxed on the first date, but it's important that you are. I like people to be open, but not confessional, for that first impression phase.

If there's a spark, you can feel it, you don't have to push anything. If you are questioning whether they're interested, then they aren't.

Back to the being relaxed thing, if I had a girlfriend who I thought was going to come across needy or desperate on a first date I would tell her to invite her girlfriends around to help her get ready. Your friends won't let you go out looking like a dog, so you'll be feeling confident that you look great. Also, being around friends does amazing things for your attitude. Shared stories, a few laughs, one wine (stress the one) … there is strength in bonding. This will all help you to approach the upcoming date in the right frame of mind. You'll arrive uplifted, relaxed, confident and the best version of yourself.

**Is it okay for girls to ask guys out?**

Yes, I think so, but I don't do that. The kind of guys I like – confident and testosterone-filled – don't need a girl to ask them out. I've learnt the hard way that if it's the right type of guy for me, I don't need to ask.

**What about sex on the first date?**

If you're only looking for a fling, go ahead. But don't whine when they don't call. Sometimes you'll hear from them and there'll be a few more dates, but it definitely takes something away from the whole experience. When they call, you're left wondering, is this a date or do they just want sex again? If you go straight to the end game with a potential partner you miss out on so much of the awesome stuff – the first kiss, the anxiety, the little bit of extra effort you both make to impress each other.

**Do you think your attitude towards dating would change if you find yourself 35-years-old, still single, and wanting children?**

No way. I don't particularly want kids, but if I come to find that I do, the world is my oyster. I don't have to be in a relationship to have kids. Single parenting is a tough route to go down, but possible. What I'm about to say is hard to do but, I believe, important – when dating you need to separate the desire to have children from the desire to fall in love, otherwise you'll negate the individual you're going on a date with.

**You seem to be quite adept at making new friends and developing a strong social circle around you when you move to a new city. How do you do it? This could be relevant for our readers who've just come out of a long-term relationship and have no single friends, but would like to make some.**

I tried online dating for friends once, but found myself out on an actual date with a girl accidentally!

I join groups in the things that I'm interested in, and pursue extracurricular work and hobbies. I do it with a view to self-development, and then just end up talking to people. If you go there with the goal of making friends, you reek of it and put people off. My most fulfilling times have happened by chance. If you're passionate about something and in your element, you attract like-minded people around you.

Definitely fake it until you make it. Push yourself out there. To do this, you have to be content with what you've got and who you are, and if you're not, then fix it. When you're happy within yourself you have a more balanced approach to making friends, and dating for that matter. When you're happy in yourself, you're more relaxed and people are more naturally drawn to you.

Never say "no" to a social invitation, and go with an open mind. You never know who you might meet while you're out. If you aren't physically out there, how are you going to bump into anyone?

If you can't go out on your own, then volunteer somewhere. This is a great way to start – you'll feel more comfortable because you'll have a purpose. Anyone who says there's nothing out there, isn't looking. Join a sport. You don't have to be training for triathlons; there are heaps of different sports out there. It's amazing the number of people I bump into at the gym.

If you're feeling desperate to find a boyfriend, I suggest that you request a friend intervention. Pick three or so friends who love you, and request that they come around and have a frank conversation. If there's something missing within yourself and you can't quite work it out, your friends will probably know what it is. Even good friends won't come out on their own volition and point these things out to you because they don't want to hurt you, but if you ask, they'll tell you. Your friends are the ones who can un-knot you, and then help you put it all back together.

I'm also a fan of counselling; not in a woe-is-me kind of way, but as an educational experience, a time for reflection about how you're putting yourself out there.

Frankly, if you have no friends and no confidence, then a love relationship isn't what you need. That breeds dependency rather than a mutual relationship. You could use a counsellor to help you work out a plan for re-building yourself.

**Whilst online dating is not your thing, do you have any tips?**

Just go for it, and commit to putting yourself out there. There may be a minority who get on it just to sleep around, but honestly, it's a lot of hard work to go to if sex is all you're looking for. You can feel relatively comfortable that most of the people you'll meet should be genuinely looking for that special someone. Be honest about who you are, use a current photo, include anything that you're passionate about. Put the work into your profile and you'll get results. But the same is true for meeting people in person, which I prefer. Put the work into finding groups/people interested in the same things you are, and you'll get results that way too.

# Author's Notes

Caroline's story is a good wake-up call for those feeling lonely and anxious about being single. When you're feeling desperate, nothing seems to go quite right. But when you're relaxed and confident, things seem to fall into place organically. If you're feeling desperate, take some time to work out why; self-reflect, heal and carve a new, considered path for your future.

I must give a word of caution if planning a 'friend intervention', as I can see opportunities for this going wrong. If you're going to do it, choose carefully the friends you ask to critique you. Ensure they are people who have sensitivity, and whose opinions and critical input you truly respect.

# Key Points From Caroline's Chapter

1. On the first few dates be open, but not confessional.
2. Adopting an attitude of never saying no to any reasonable social invitation opens you up to some surprisingly delightful encounters that you might otherwise miss out on.
3. When you're happy within yourself, you have a more balanced, relaxed approach to making new friends and dating, and people are more naturally drawn to you.

# Chapter 9

## Andrea's Story

**Trapped in a needy relationship for over seven years, 39-years-old and an Office Manager, Andrea is genuine, intelligent and articulate. Her eyes sparkle and she's fun, warm and open. She's also just spent a large part of her life battling to overcome her demons. As with most people, her 'layers' hold the story.**

What are my character traits? What an interesting way to start an interview. I guess I'm funny, resilient, a survivor, energetic, intuitive, thoughtful, I can be negative, judgemental of others, quirky, loving, affectionate, a daydreamer, lively, active, fit, awesome, contradictory, silly, enduring, wise, dumb, egotistical, self-critical, outside-the-box, a non-conformer who tries to be a conformer but it just doesn't work. I could never put myself into any one category. I'm also the daughter of an alcoholic. I'm a recovering alcoholic who has now been sober for nine years.

My first relationship lasted four years, but he was an alcoholic and I didn't want an alcoholic father for my children. I left him when I was 23-years-old.

For the next nine years I travelled a lot; drinking and drugging heavily.

I come from a dysfunctional, broken home. My father was an alcoholic and he treated my Mum horrendously. I have major trust issues towards men. My friends were settling down, but I was still partying, having flings with men. I couldn't find my niche and I felt terribly unloved. I denied myself love because I didn't feel like I was worthy. I had a great body but I didn't want anybody to see me naked. I felt an all-pervasive shame and I couldn't stop drinking. I also had bulimia for years.

I tried to 'find' myself in a monkery for three months. There, I ate myself sick. I did everything in extremes. Can't fault my commitment.

I went to Perth when I was 25-years-old and had an amazing month-long affair with a Canadian artist. He told his Mum about me and wanted me to go back to Canada with him, but I was too fearful to make such a big move.

At 26 I knew I needed to get well. I started going back to church, looking for God. I'm a Seventh Day Adventist and I find church to be a source of solace and strength.

My sister was sober and she was encouraging me to do the same. One night, I woke up in bed with a stranger, covered in bruises and he knew my whole life story. It was a water-shed moment. I saw two paths in front of me – death or sobriety. I phoned my sister. I was 30 when Alcoholics Anonymous helped me get sober.

I had always thought that once I got sober, my life would be 'sorted'. But when I finally got there, I realised the real struggle had only just begun. Alcoholism is a three-fold disease: mental, spiritual and physical. Sober, I realised the damage I had inflicted on myself and my family for the previous ten years. These realisations were confronting and far worse than anything else I had been through before.

AA has got a strong program and once I attended meetings I started getting well.

I met Shaun in an AA meeting when I was 32. At first I wasn't interested in him. He was older and had that air about him that happily married men get. But then we had a couple of nice interactions at meetings, and I found out he was single and he asked me out on a date. He had recently been dumped by a married woman who was in an abusive relationship with her husband. Shaun thought she was the love his life and he was devastated by the break-up.

He went straight into a relationship with me, while he was broken-hearted over her. After six months he asked me to move in with him. He told me he'd never lived with anyone other than his former wife. I didn't move in straight away, something was deterring me, but eventually I capitulated.

Looking back now from a position of hindsight, there was a red flag to what was to come, but at the time I overlooked it. On our first date he texted me a racy message about how far I was prepared to go down on him. I'm not a prude, but I thought it was a little off for so early in a relationship. But then we went for coffee and had this amazing connection and a wonderful time together.

We had this wonderfully romantic couple of years and I loved him. I wanted to marry him. He told me he didn't want children, but I had this fantasy that once you meet the right person and fall in love all that changes, that you just naturally want to have children together.

After the first two years, I discovered he had slept around on me. I ended the relationship.

He called a couple of weeks later and said he really loved me and wanted to be with me. We re-united a few months later. I was still very much in love with him and I convinced myself that his affair was just an oversight and that I would be able to forgive him. I raised the topic of marriage and he said he would ask me in his own time when he was ready.

We walked, cooked and read together. We wrote stories to each other. It was romantic and beautiful and I thought we were building a life together. He taught me to drive. However, it dented my happiness that he was always working and never seemed to be able to come to my family events with me.

Things were good for a while, then one day I had an instinct to look up a particular online dating site. I knew he'd been on there while we were broken up. Sure enough, he still had a profile up. When I confronted him, he said he put it up to show a friend how to do it. He even called his friend and had his friend confirm it to me. I didn't believe them, however he took it down.

Shaun was a recovered alcoholic just like me. I believe that when alcoholics are not medicating themselves with alcohol, they need to have a spiritual program in their life or they will revert to functioning in the disease. He didn't tend to his spiritual garden so sometimes even though he wasn't drinking, it felt like I was living with an alcoholic because he was cranky and irritable. However, he adored me, loved me, bought me presents, wrote me poems, and we had amazing sex together.

He drove the relationship; making all the decisions. He worked out where we were going to go and what we were going to eat. I loved that. It was easy.

After about two years things started getting rocky and we began to argue. I wanted commitment and I felt he wasn't fully committed to me. I could sense he was flirting with women in the background.

Looking back, I realise that I made him the father and God in our relationship, and I was the little girl. Even though he wanted the power, he also came to resent it. I had poor communication skills; I didn't know how to speak up and express my needs. Our relationship was all about his world: his restaurants that he owned, him making money.

Then I found a text message on his phone from his ex-girlfriend. He told me she contacted him because she was trying to get sober and she wanted him to be her sponsor. I was uncomfortable with this and suggested that there was a world-wide network, and she could find someone else, not my boyfriend. He then confessed he had never stopped thinking about her and asked me to move out.

They didn't last long together. It was only a short time later that he told me that she left him.

He and I then slept together on and off for the next six months, until I found out that he was sleeping with her too. We broke up again.

We remained in contact so when he went to New York for a month-long holiday, he asked me to look after his restaurant for him. He returned on my birthday with heaps of presents for me and we got back together again. He was moving house at the time and because of his work commitments, I offered to pack up his house for him. While doing this, I found his journal and discovered that he had taken his ex to New York with him. I couldn't believe he had so blatantly lied to me and taken advantage of me to look after his restaurant.

I broke up with him … *again* … and we didn't speak to each other for eleven months.

Then he emailed me on my birthday, and after a few emails back and forth we went to a concert together. We got back together and went to America for an amazing five-week holiday. He said he wanted to have a child with me. I moved out of my home, and back into his house. I was living in the country with the man I loved and a vegetable patch. I had never been happier in my life. And then something changed, and I can't tell you what it was.

I asked him when we were going to get married and he told me to stop pressuring him. That triggered my feelings that I wasn't good enough for him. I sensed he was flirting with other women again, perhaps sleeping with someone, and we started fighting again. There was a part of his life that he always kept closed from me. We had a fight and he threw a bottle of Gatorade at me, smashing a picture. I'd never seen him that angry before and it scared me. These rages had been building for a while. He once went nuts at me for leaving the back door open. I told him his anger wasn't in proportion to what I'd done but he didn't want to talk about it.

I left and moved to another town.

Then a friend of ours died and Shaun got in contact with me again. Every time we got together we got on great at first. The conversation and sexual chemistry was amazing. We got together a few times, but I could feel that we were slowly separating from each other. I still had hope that we would eventually end up together. But then I phoned him to share with him that I had just received my first distinction at college, and he mentioned that he was going to Borneo in a couple of days for a 10-day holiday, and it was the first I had heard about it. I realised that he didn't even see me as his girlfriend, let alone consider himself committed to me.

I went on a holiday to Nepal as a healing endeavour for myself. Before I left, I told him I was desperately in love with him but I didn't know what to do because we never seemed to work when we lived together. When I returned from my holiday, he was seeing someone else. In a moment of clarity, I realised I had been in a relationship with him for seven years, but he had been in a relationship with me for only half that time.

I've now been single for six months and I'm still in pain and grief. I'm questioning my worth and whether or not I really do want marriage and kids. I realise that at 39 years of age it could go either way.

I feel a sense of freedom and gratitude towards my ex's current girlfriend. My AA sponsor always said that the best thing Shaun could do for me was to meet someone else. I'm starting to be objective about it, which means I'm healing quicker this time than ever before. I also understand myself better now. This relationship with Shaun was my search for my Father. When my Dad died, I was drunk and high and never let myself grieve. Now I feel like I'm grieving the loss of Shaun and the loss of my Dad at the same time. There's also a purifying feeling; like all the demons are being purged at once.

I'm now exploring what it is within me that made me place so little value on myself.

I put myself on a singles fitness website, and I got a message from a guy last week, but I didn't reply. I'm just not quite ready. I think I'll be interested in dating again soon, but it'll be difficult to open my heart up to possible hurt.

I'm still in the angry stage at this point. I'm still fantasising about running into Shaun while I'm with my new husband. I look amazing and so does my new husband and my ex regrets everything he ever did to me.

**What is working to help you heal?**

1. Time with girlfriends.
2. Having male friends who love me and tell me I'm attractive because they genuinely care about me.
3. Having other men compliment me. This reinforces that I'm not 'past it'. When you are with someone who is constantly with other women it does something to your self-esteem.
4. Paddle boarding with groups of friends.
5. Watching Sex in the City and eating ice cream.

**Are you concerned that there are few good single men in your age bracket?**

No, I've never lost faith that relationships work and I still have that belief that there is a relationship for me. I only need one single man; there's got to be at least one out there on the same wavelength as me! I believe I'll meet someone spontaneously. There are heaps of good guys who go to running club.

**What have you learnt about relationships?**

1. They're not perfect; even the good ones.
2. Relationships need nurturing and effort; they require work.
3. You must have trust.
4. If you're putting too much work into the relationship, there's something wrong.

**How will you recognise who is going to be good for you next time around?**

1. Not ignore early warning signs that make me feel uncomfortable.
2. Hopefully, all the work I've put in over the last few years will be my foundation and my guiding stick. I've been to therapy, entered programs, read books, looked at myself, and haven't rushed into another relationship too soon.

**What are your hopes for the future?**

1. Finish my Masters in Counselling. I'm mostly doing this degree as an insight into my own life and for character development in my writing.
2. Write a book; it's always been my goal to write.
3. Meet somebody and fall in love.
4. Keep travelling.
5. Continue doing volunteer work. I've always worked with adolescents and I'm a sponsor in my AA group. I've helped at camps for teenagers, a soup kitchen, and I recently volunteered for two weeks in an orphanage in Nepal.

I'm not unhappy you know. I've done some amazing things in my life. But I'm just not where I want to be. The next man I fall in love with will be committed, faithful, honest and have integrity. I'm working on my communication skills in order to be able to express my needs in a relationship.

Growing up in an alcoholic home everything is focussed around the alcoholic and his needs. It's a monster that you don't want to upset because the wrath is too great. We grew up with three golden rules: don't talk, don't feel, and don't rock the boat. I'm unravelling this foundation in order to create a new one.

**9 Months Later**

It's now been over nine months since the interview with the author. I didn't realise at the time that she was asking for people who had found love the second time around. I had been so stuck in my grief and turmoil that I couldn't have seen beyond my pain. However, she was gracious enough to not only hear my story, but to hold it in this sacred space of empathy, understanding and kindness, and then to tell it.

When I read what she'd written, I cried. Never had anyone heard my story so well, and told it so beautifully. Turning this ugly mess into something fragile and beautiful. Carolyn articulated the threads that brought it all into a story that I couldn't tell myself.

She asked me to write you a letter – *Dear Reader* – to tell you what happened afterwards.

At the time of the break up, I thought that it would take me years to get over Shaun and years to find love again. I felt so bruised, so damaged, so broken that I didn't think I could ever let anyone near me again.

One thing people kept telling me was that to get over one relationship, you need to find another. This philosophy left me cold and flew in the face of my counselling background. Healing time is required to get over the grief and loss; it takes serious work and long-term therapy. Going headlong into a new relationship was merely putting a bandaid on the gaping wound; a placebo to heal the pain. "You need a good shag," was the other piece of advice I received from well-meaning friends who had clearly not been as deeply hurt as I had.

But for the first time in the entire seven long and boring years during which we had broken up, got back together, he had cheated, lied, promised, crawled back, I left a job, house, got my life back together, to only have it wrecked again ... I was tired. I was tired of the cycle, tired of hurting and not moving on in my life toward what I wanted – which was a partner to share my life with and a family of my own.

I decided that I was going to be proactive. In the past, I'd always let the men choose me; I'd never actually had a choice in who I was with. In the past, someone would show me some interest and I was so starved of love and self-esteem, that I jumped at the little crumbs that were offered me. Mind you, they were grand gestures in the beginning, always grand gestures that turned to crumbs once the conquest was won.

Online dating had never appealed to me, I thought it for desperados who couldn't meet anyone the normal way. But here was I, 39-years-old, single, a sober alcoholic, a Christian … there were conditions that came with me, damage clauses. It's true that no-one gets to 40 without carrying their own set of baggage. So what did I think made me so different? I don't know really – pride, my history ... although I hear worse, much, much worse.

I was proud, full of expectation and entitlement. I was a nice girl after all, hard done by. Why not me?

I did do the therapy, I did do the grieving, I did do the crying and ice cream and I did do the online dating.

I just decided, I was 39, I didn't want to wait around for Mr Right to walk in my front door. I once read a story from a well-known psychologist who was talking to a woman who truly believed that God would bring her husband to the front door. He turned around to her and said, "Well, unless you want to marry the FedEx man, it ain't gonna happen." It was a light bulb moment for me, clearly showing me the difference between my childish expectations and the reality.

I had to be proactive to some degree but I wasn't going to go via the normal mainstream internet dating sites. I liked running, so I went on to a Fitness Singles site to meet a running buddy. To be honest, I just wanted something to distract me from the pain. I was having daily panic attacks on the way to work, so much that I had to pull over and cry and breathe until they passed. This went on for months. I had to do something.

So I put up a profile. It was honest, it was exactly what I wanted to say and it was not 'nicey nice'. I didn't try to sell myself. I didn't put up any 'hot' photos. Just nice photos that I thought said who I was. Photos where I looked happy; running photos.

A few guys emailed, boring stuff like, "Wanna hook up?", "Nice smile wanna hook up?" ... "Like your profile, do you like mine?" ... I didn't get a great deal of hits. It was funny, I looked at the *Top 10 Female Profiles* once … they were the 'hot' girls. Lots of hot photos, tits, tight tops, hot bodies, pretty in a nasty kinda way, botox ... ugh. Wow, if this was my competition I thought, no wonder I'm not getting much action.

I'm not bad looking, I've never been short of male interest. I think I'm just wary. Some may say picky. Picky becomes boring and lonely after a while.

Then I got an email that stopped me in my tracks. It went along the lines of, "Nice to see a bit of honesty ... and ... I may not have all the answers, but would love to discover some of them with you". He finished with, "Would like to get to know you better".

And that was it. We emailed back and forth for about three months. They were not deep, emotional, intellectual exchanges, but there was something honest and raw and wholesome in our conversations. There was also something light and free and happy. I felt this sense of ease with him and this incredible sense of having time. There was no rush from the very beginning. It was slow, but it was definite. I had no reservations that he was interested.

After a few months, he still hadn't asked me out and I wondered if he was actually interested or if he was dating or finishing up with someone else. Then, out of the blue, he asked if I wanted to go out for coffee and sent me his mobile number. I texted him the next morning, we made a date and met. It was a rainy Sunday morning and he had just completed a 21km training run as he was training for a marathon. I was impressed.

I can't quite explain it, but when he walked into the café that day, I knew it was him. Our eyes met as soon as we were in view of each other and I felt a thousand years between us already, and I knew him already.

When he sat down though, I thought … umm, first and only date. He was so not my type. So not! He dressed like my older brother, God bless him (sorry bro, I adore you, but you're not a style monger by any means). I didn't think he was handsome at all. He was shorter than I'd imagined and somehow looked older, he had a bald patch in the middle of his head and wore a red fleece and sneakers with jeans; not cool sneakers, runners.

But then he took off his jacket and I noticed these beautiful eyes, and he had a very nice blue and white striped polo top on. He looked very French. Funny the things that bias you.

When I look into Nathan's eyes, I see my future. I've never seen that before with anyone. And even as I write this, I can't tell you if it's love the second time around, because with Nathan, it feels like my first love. It's dizzying and intoxicating and wonderful and the passion between us is like nothing, nothing I have ever experienced. But best of all, he makes me feel safe. I trust him absolutely, and there is no question about that.

He sees me, he doesn't need to compete with me; we're equal. He teaches me things, how to be less complicated, how to be in the present moment. He encourages me, we encourage and support each other. He finds me incredibly sexy. He makes me feel like I'm the only one in the world for him.

Within a few months of dating, it was clear we were both head over heels in love. The difference in being with Nathan to being with Shaun is incredible. I don't feel any desperate desire for him to marry me or have children. I want to spend time discovering him and I know he's committed to me already, in his heart and mind and soul.

Funnily enough, I still miss Shaun and have just gone through another grieving period over him. He did have some great things about him and we shared things neither of us will share with anyone else. I miss that stuff. He was my first love in sobriety and in some ways he was my father, my teacher and at times my Higher Power. Somewhere inside, I always knew it would end and he wasn't the one, but I resisted it for a long time because he did fill those roles.

I don't think there is The One. I'm not a believer in the one myth or philosophy. What I think now is that you choose someone who equals you in body, mind, spirit and in the bedroom, and someone with whom it's easy, no messy complications, and someone who is available, emotionally and physically.

Nathan and I haven't spoken about our exes to each other, only that there has been hurt and that they are exes for a reason. We're so happy for it just to be us at the moment. It's fun with him, it's beautiful, it's rich and fulfilling. It's gentle and passionate. We write to each other every day, we tell each other how we feel every day. We respect each other's lives, each other's need for space. We have met each other's families and both like each other's families.

I don't know where it will go. For the first time in my life, I'm not concerned about the future. I'm free in who I am. I've done the work and there is more work to come. I know that there is more grief and pain and sadness, because this is life after all. But today is what I have and today is glorious and happy and full of hope. Nathan is teaching me how to live in the moment. As a result, I'm experiencing this delicate, amazing intimacy for the first time in my life.

# Author's Notes

Humans are complex beings. I think most can relate to Andrea when she describes herself as opposites "silly, enduring, wise and dumb". Life is complex. At times, it is beneficial to peel back the layers and evaluate where and who you are, and where and who you want to be. Are you being true to yourself? Are you accepting less than you deserve in any aspect of your life? Andrea found it confronting, revealing and eventually liberating to read her story following our interview. She saw herself in a light that she'd never seen before. When she had the benefit of reading her story, she realised that Shaun was never going to change. He was who he was. Vivid patterns emerged that were there all along, but during the relationship Andrea was too 'close' to see them. A leopard doesn't change its spots.

If, like Andrea, you need help overcoming or managing something in your life, seek out that help. Seeing a counsellor, for instance, is not a sign of weakness. It's a sign that you have the strength and grace to seek further education. Counselling is not about 'fixing' you because you are 'broken'. Counselling is simply another way to learn better communication and other life skills. In life, we should never stop learning. That Andrea identifies she still needs male friends to tell her she's attractive demonstrates that she's still on the path of rebuilding her self-esteem.

Vincent Van Gogh once said, "Great things are not done by impulse, but by a series of small things brought together." Peeling away the layers can be likened to this.

# Key Points From Andrea's Chapter

1. Don't ignore early warning signs that make you feel uncomfortable.
2. There are internet dating sites such as Fitness Singles which you can utilise to meet like-minded people. It's worth researching to see what's out there.
3. Taking a step back and evaluating your experiences with potential suitors is a good habit to practise. Use your head as well as your other senses.

# Chapter 10

## Dan's Story

**34-year-old Dan offers a candid conversation around allowing circumstances to choose your partner versus consciously choosing a partner suited to you. Share his journey as he discusses how he 'fell' into his first marriage, and the detrimental impact this had. He ends with some practical tips for singles.**

In my early twenties, I was in the army and met Joanna. We were on a field exercise and we were both engaged to other people. You get to know people quickly when you're in a barracks situation – eating, sleeping, working together. Joanna and I had become close, but we weren't in a physical relationship.

One night Joanna asked if she could sleep in the back of my truck where I was sleeping. I said "no" so she slept in the front cab instead. That was enough though, because of that incident, people talked. It spread like wildfire that there was something going on between us. Her fiancé was in the army too and the talk made its way back to him.

After the 3-month exercise, it was my job to drop everyone back to their homes. When we got to Joanna's unit, I helped her inside with her things. When I walked in, I could smell gunpowder. Joanna didn't notice at first. I looked around and found her fiancé inside the walk-in robe. He'd committed suicide. There was nothing between Joanna and I, but he thought there was because of the rumours. I will never forget the look on her face when I told her. I stopped her going into the room, and called triple 0.

The media arrived before the police did. It became a circus. There was a police investigation into the death and I was the number one suspect for about three weeks. Joanna and I were the only ones who knew the truth. I lost all my mates from that unit. Joanna left the army.

I hated authority after that. I'd always wanted to join the army and later become a police officer, but after those experiences I changed my mind. The police went to the army barracks and spoke to people before I even made it home after the triple 0 call, so they heard the rumours and treated me quite badly. I answered their questions in a straight-forward manner. It was an awful experience.

I loved my fiancé, Tanya, very much, but the rumour mill was so vicious that I felt she deserved better than me after everything that unfolded, and I ended our relationship.

I got posted to the army base in Darwin and demoted from driving double articulated low loaders and transport tanks to driving a basic truck instead. Officially, it was a routine transfer, but unofficially I understood it as a form of punishment.

You know that saying, "If you're getting blamed for something you may as well be doing it"? I guess the next period in my life can be somewhat summarised by that saying. I honestly tried hard for nothing to happen between Joanna and I. After her fiancé's suicide she leant on me for support. I think it started from the way I made the triple 0 call, and how I kept everyone at bay in the aftermath, and tried to protect her from the media. I took her under my wing. She went through a lot: losing her fiancé to suicide, the gossip, and leaving the army. When I got posted to Darwin she drove up with me to see her brother, who lived up there.

We "got together" on that drive, and moved in together when we arrived in Darwin. We later got married, with her brother and a mate of mine as witnesses.

We got along well in Darwin, although our relationship was a little volatile. Neither of us knew anyone there so we did everything together and there were no major complications, but we argued about the day-to-day things.

After fourteen months in Darwin, I left the army. Cashed up from my payout, we moved interstate and built our dream home. Joanna didn't have any reason not to trust me, but she started having trust issues with me. If I was late home from work I'd get a grilling. We started arguing a lot.

We made new friends and Joanna started coming out of her shell. Then our child, Anna, was born.

The fighting and trust issues didn't abate. I was late getting home on Joanna's birthday because I stopped to buy her a present. When I got through the door and got an ear bashing I threw her present and moved out for a few months. I'd had enough.

She then moved interstate again, so I moved back into the house with a mate to finish off the landscaping so we could sell it. Joanna suggested she keep the house in lieu of me paying maintenance. I agreed and we had an amicable split. I actually thought we would talk and eventually get back together, but then she called one day and asked if I minded if she started seeing someone, and I realised I didn't mind at all.

After Joanna and I broke up I moved into a party house full of blokes in their early 20s. I was older so I was the father figure, although I wasn't particularly good at being a responsible role model. There was a lot of typical male fun in that house – much drinking.

I met Kym at a mate's 21st in the country. She and I were both playing soccer with the kids in the backyard. We were the last people to go to bed that night. We sat around a fire and talked and talked and talked. It was like we had known each other forever. I remember thinking, "This is good, this is the way it's supposed to be". I genuinely found her interesting.

I took two extra days off work and spent time with her. We hung out and talked.

After I returned home, Kym and I spoke for hundreds of hours on the phone before we got to physically see each other again because of the distance. When we did finally get to see each other, we held hands and kissed, and I bought her flowers when she got back on the train. I fell in love with her the day I met her. She was my best mate. I just loved what she did, how she held herself, the way she interacted with kids, the way she did everything. She was a female version of me. I was worried because I was seven years older than her and I thought her parents would disapprove, but it turned out that there was a seven-year age gap in their marriage too.

Getting married a second time wasn't an issue for me because I knew why my first marriage didn't work. Circumstances pushed us together, but we weren't right for each other. I still thought marriage was a beautiful thing. Kym and I were right for each other.

When you're married to the wrong person, it's a chore – things don't flow, and you have to lie to yourself about how happy you are. You aren't yourself. When you truly fall in love with the right person for you, there is no false façade. You are effortlessly attentive towards each other, respectful and interested in each other's conversation. With some people, it's easy to be in a conversation, but not really care and not really listen. When it's 'the one', you listen to everything they say. There's no forcing the issue; you simply know you've met your best friend and you can share things with this person that you wouldn't share with anyone else.

**How can a woman recognise when a man is into them?**

I guess it's important for women to understand that guys will chase any girl for sex. Any guy will chase a woman in a short skirt and heels.

If a guy is truly into a woman, he'll be attentive and listen to what they say. There will be a build up of touching and kissing.

I'm a romantic at heart. I like the whole journey, the awkwardness. I want to experience it all, and not just jump from A to Z and miss out on all the good stuff in between.

**What are the secrets to a successful marriage?**

1. The ability to talk things through. Every long-term relationship has its ups and downs, but so long as you can talk things through, you'll be fine.
2. Understanding of each other's alone time. Despite being a couple you still need single time, or time with other people, and you have got to allow each other to have that.
3. Patience.
4. When you're going through a rough patch, remember why you fell for them in the first place.
5. Respect for each other.
6. Trust; if you don't have trust, you've got major issues. Even if you have everything else, it won't work without trust.
7. Similar Personal Values and views, especially when raising kids. Things like religious views, smacking, etc, become quite important once you have kids.
8. You can't be pigheaded, stubborn or think that everything is going to be perfect all the time.

**What advice would you give a mate who is lonely and struggling to meet the type of woman he wants to date?**

1. Be patient; it'll happen. I've seen people who've said they'll never meet someone, and then they just do. You meet the girl version of you, and it just happens. I believe in meeting someone by chance; I'm not a fan of searching. If you're doing the same thing over and over and it isn't working, then simply do something different.
2. Women are not everything; there is still life to be had. Play touch footy with your mates.
3. People need to take care of their physical and emotional health before they get into a relationship.
4. Start doing something you're interested in. For instance, take up running. You'll hate it for two or three weeks, but when you get past that point, it feels great. When you do something that makes you feel good about yourself, things seem to pick up in other areas of your life too.
5. Friends are a massively important part of life. You must have at least one really good, true, dependable friend.

**What are the best ways to meet people while you're single?**

Chance is best. You've got to pick your venue though. For instance, if you're a pub or an RSL type of person then meeting someone there is fine, but what's the point of picking up there if you aren't that type of person? Chances are your new partner is going to want to go there regularly, and it's going to be a problem if you aren't really into it. Sport is a good way of interacting with and meeting people. Again, I wouldn't pick a sport that you aren't interested in, but a sport you are interested in is a good place to start.

Also, you need a wingman to give you a second opinion. If you're looking for a relationship, you might take the first person who comes along. A wingman helps give you perspective. The ultimate wingman is someone of the opposite sex – they give a different perspective. A wingman doesn't always have to go out with you; they could simply be the person that you run things past for a second opinion.

I tell all the single girls who ask me for advice that they need to be aware of how they're dressed when a guy picks them up. If they're dressed in a short skirt and heels any guy is going to be charming to get sex. If he's got a condom in his pocket, get rid of him – he's looking for a one-night stand, not a relationship.

A friend once told me that a guy she liked didn't ask her out until he saw her in her skimpy, lycra, running gear. I told her to forget him. What's the point in dating a guy who didn't show any interest in her until he saw her in a leotard?

**What do you think women generally need to work on in relationships?**

I think they need to understand that inside the house is not all they need to consider in terms of job sharing around the house. A guy can spend four hours of his Saturday doing the mowing, hedging, etc. and then come inside and his wife whinges at him that he doesn't do anything! You need to understand each other's roles and who is doing what. At the end of the day, you can rip someone apart when you don't value something that is important to them.

**What do you think men generally need to work on in relationships?**

Communication, understanding that once kids come along he can't be first anymore, and helping more. For instance, I know guys who watch their wives doing the mundane, kids things for a couple of hours, and then wonder why their wife doesn't have any time for them anymore. If they got up and helped her, instead of watching, it would be an hour of work, not two.

**What things should single women understand about men while dating?**

1. Men are not all the same. You can't judge one guy for what another guy has done to you.
2. Different men are looking for different things. For instance, I think women fall in love when they meet 'the one'. It's different for guys. We could meet 'the one' but if we aren't ready to settle down, then we won't. We won't settle down unless we're at a point in our life that it suits us to do so. So, if you meet a party guy who is obviously more interested in going out with his mates than spending time with you, don't think that is going to change any time soon. It won't.
3. Mateship is a bond that guys don't break just to run off with another girl.
4. Guys need to be trusted. Acting jealous isn't going to stop a guy sleeping around – it's probably more likely to make it happen. Trust is vitally important in a marriage. As is healthy communication. Good, satisfying communication within the marriage minimises the risk of one partner becoming more 'connected' on any particular topic to a person outside the marriage, than to their partner. It's a dangerous place if your partner constantly picks on you about something, but someone outside your marriage admires that aspect of your personality or character. We all know life throws us curveballs; eg. an unexpected death in the family, losing all your money in a stock market crash, being made redundant at work – it's important that couples communicate lovingly and healthily through everything that comes their way to maintain that strong connection to their 'best friend'.
5. Guys need some time to themselves. It's energising to come home and have interesting conversation to share with your partner.

# Author's Notes

Dan's story is a poignant example of what can occur when we allow circumstances to write our love life. Reflect on who you are, what kind of love relationship you want in your life, and the qualities and Personal Values that any prospective partner will need to have to match you.

At one point in his narrative Dan says that he prefers to meet people by chance, but then he goes on to say that his single mates should join activities and groups that they are interested in. So he does in fact have a strategy! Leaving things to chance may not reap the results you seek. There are actions you can take to maximise your chances of meeting suitable contenders for the title of your next partner.

# Key Points From Dan's Chapter

1. If your desire is to meet people by chance, then it helps to get involved in activities that increase the probability of meeting a person with similar interests.
2. Similar Personal Values are critically important to ongoing success in a relationship.
3. Be aware of how you present yourself to potential partners.

# Chapter 11

## Stacey's Story

**Loneliness following a significant relationship breakdown is a commonly experienced emotion. 45-year-old Stacey has a solid remedy.**

The first six weeks after my break-up were tragic. At the time I made the decision to leave my husband, I was confident that I was doing the right thing but six weeks later I felt old, negative, inadequate, and thought I'd never meet anyone ever again. I actually called my ex-husband up, but of course, it was never going to work. We broke up for a reason.

I felt I needed to get away so I decided to travel to Italy and Greece on my own. However, as people heard of my plans, opportunities for company presented themselves. I ended up going to France to watch my Dad play tennis. I then backpacked up the Nile on my own for 12 days. Following this, I met one of my daughters in Rome and we flew to Venice together. Venice is my favourite place, a city of romance, so to be there with my daughter instead of a love interest was in some ways challenging, but we had such a great time together. We laughed a lot. We tried 37 different flavours of gelato, and hired a luxurious Alfa Romeo for nine nights and drove through the countryside of Florence, Pisa, Siena,

San Gimignano, Sorrento and the Isle of Capri. It was liberating, fun, beautiful and an incredibly special adventure to share with my daughter.

By the time I returned home I was strong again, and young.

Looking back over my marriage break-up, one of the best things I did was to leave my past behind me. When my youngest daughter left home, I bought all new furniture that reflected just my personality and tastes, and moved into a 2-bedroom villa that was the right size for me. My new environment definitely helped me 'find' myself and move on – I was no longer surrounded by memories. It was wonderful having my own space, and being a small villa it didn't break the bank.

When my step-brother passed away suddenly at the age of 42, I realised life was too short to have walls around me. I was reminded of the words of one of my favorite songs, *Last Thing I Wanna Do* by McAlister Kemp.

So with that I adopted what I call the *Arms Wide Open* approach. I vowed to embrace life and every new opportunity with arms wide open.

With that new attitude, I formed a private Facebook group for singles only. It started out as just a handful of us who were single, and gradually members invited others to join. Now there are about 25 men and women in the group. If I feel like going to a movie or the beach or anywhere else and I would like some company, I post on the site my plans and ask who wants to go along. There is always someone in the group with a good suggestion for something to do, and when you post an invite yourself, you always get at least one other, usually more, who want to go along with you. We regularly catch up for BBQs and drinks as the full group. We are a great support for each other. None of us is sitting at home wishing we had someone to go out with.

We made sure the Facebook group was a Closed Group with membership by invitation only. Every new friend seems to have another good friend who is single. It works well. Because it's an established friends network we largely seem to have similar Personal Values and interests. That's important I believe. I've made wonderful new friends through the group.

Now my dilemma is, what do I do when I fall in love again? My singles group is quite terrific; I wouldn't want to lose them (laughs).

## Author's Notes

Stacey is proof that with a little ingenuity you can tailor experiences around you to suit your individual circumstances. Many Finding Love interviewees discuss joining groups in their interest area. If such a group isn't available to you, start one.

# Key Points From Stacey's Chapter

1. Move on from old memories and make new ones.
2. Embrace every new reasonable opportunity that comes your way with arms wide open.
3. Like people attract like people. Join a group, or start a group.

# Chapter 12

### Jack's Story

**Grief never ends, but it changes. 78-year-old Jack is well known in his home town, having owned an iconic pub for many years. His forthright, positive, calm and grateful outlook on life is evident as he shares what it was like to lose his much-loved wife of 40 years. He eloquently shares how and why he fell in love again as he takes us on a journey of a life well spent.**

Julie-Anna and I had been married for 40 years when she passed away on 5 August 1999. She loved me and the kids tremendously.

We were about to go away on holidays, and Julie-Anna started sounding like she was drunk when she tried to say certain words, like "linen" for example. We went to the doctor, but he said it wasn't serious and suggested we continue with our holiday plans. So we did. New York and London for three fabulous weeks. But Julie-Anna got anxious while we were away – she knew within herself that it was something serious. When we returned home, she was diagnosed with Motor Neurone Disease. It is an awful, awful disease.

Leaving the doctor's office after that diagnosis was the first time in my life that I was flummoxed. We knew straight away that it was a death sentence. My vibrant wife was 61-years-old, and we had just been told that she might have a couple of years left. She would lose her speech and her hand movements. Her mind would remain strong but as the disease progressed she wouldn't be able to express herself.

My wife … Julie-Anna was attractive and intelligent. Our marriage was tumultuous at times, but a very good marriage. We were different people with different points of view so we had our problems occasionally just like everyone does in an honest relationship. We only truly argued over two things – differences in opinions on the things we were both most passionate about – how to raise the four kids, and how to run the pub. Early in our career, we sold our house to buy the pub so it was a big deal for both of us.

Usually, when you have a problem in a marriage it isn't because either one is right or wrong, it's just that you've got different points of view. Julie-Anna was a very passionate person, and a very good mother. We went to a couple of psychologists over the years – a third person can sometimes help you to reach a healthy compromise when you reach a sticking point in a marriage. I found that Julie-Anna had a dismal sense of timing – she had a knack for approaching me with the wrong thing at the wrong time, and no doubt I frustrated the hell out of her sometimes too.

Julie-Anna and I liked shopping, watching the tele, going to Sydney to see shows, the pictures, and travelling together. Because we were so very busy at the pub, we liked to relax when we did get a moment together, hence the tele was a good off-switch for us.

In life, I've made some good decisions, but I've also been lucky. When we decided to sell the pub, people were telling me not to sell because pokies were coming in, but I knew it was the right time for us. And then Julie-Anna was diagnosed not long after we sold. I could never have managed Julie-Anna's illness and the pub at the same time. My business partner also died within 15 months of us selling the pub. There is no way I could have handled all that while running the popular hotel.

There is really no idyllic situation in life; you make your own luck. I was lucky to marry the woman I did, but I also made sure that I married someone who was right for me, and together we raised a good family, and worked a successful business.

When Julie-Anna was diagnosed with Motor Neurone Disease, she was accepting of it. She didn't like it; but she accepted it. Julie-Anna was a very good person, and if someone in our family had to get sick, she preferred that it be her than one of our kids, and that's how she rationalised her illness, and how she came to terms with it.

We always liked to view every situation in the most positive light possible – we considered ourselves lucky that we had just sold the pub. I looked after her at home as her illness progressed, and together we set about finishing the renovations we had started at home shortly after selling the business.

About a month before Julie-Anna died, I got a new hospital bed installed at home so she would be comfortable. One day, we'd had a really good afternoon with our daughter and some cousins; a drink and a talk, and then that night Julie-Anna couldn't get comfortable in bed. We decided to call the hospice the next day and ask for some pain management. It's funny, they (the hospital) seemed to know. Before I called them, they called me and offered us a bed. I promised Julie-Anna I would bring her home again, but then she got an infection, and she went downhill fast. I spent that month by her side, sleeping on a stretcher near her bed. Morphine is a funny thing – you need it, but it also assists your demise. I would have hated to see Julie-Anna suffer any more than she did. She was diagnosed with the disease at 61, and died at 62.

After she died, I was in the bedroom putting her clothes away that night and my granddaughter put on a CD. Funnily enough the first song to come on was the one we'd chosen for the funeral. It was a beautiful hymn, and it felt like Julie-Anna picked it especially for me to hear in that moment. Shortly after I went to bed, my son Paul phoned and said he'd just seen a shooting star. All our family felt her around us that night. It gave me strength. I can't prove it, but I have known since that night that there is a better place than where we are here, and Julie-Anna is there.

There is absolutely no doubt, I missed Julie-Anna, but when you're pragmatic there's no point in getting shitty about life. You need to move on. Of course you grieve. When someone dies the way Julie-Anna died, you do much of your grieving while they're dying. When you see someone in so much pain, you just want their pain to end. When they finally go, you're happy for them.

I was 64 when Julie-Anna died.

I wasn't terribly lonely because my eldest daughter and my granddaughter lived with me for some time. When they left, my other daughter moved in for a while. They weren't there to do anything for me; it suited them all at the time because of things going on in their own lives. One was renovating their house, the other one needed to get back on their feet financially so rented their own house out for a while and lived with me while they re-grouped. Them being there worked for all of us – for me, it meant I wasn't lonely during what would otherwise have been quite a lonely time.

I knew a lot of people, and I did get some invitations after Julie-Anna died, but to be perfectly honest, I knocked them back. I wasn't interested in any extra social activities outside my normal routine and time with my family.

My son called one day and asked if I would like to join him for a drink with the Captain – a friend of ours who'd had a stroke. There was a group of people there, and Lorraine was one of them. Funnily enough, my sister used to socialise with her – and they would often go to the football together.

I walked Lorraine home. As we walked away, the Captain said to the others, "Look at the widow bloke walking the widow woman home."

I thought Lorraine was an interesting and attractive woman so I called her up and asked if she would like to go see the Christmas lights in Sydney. I figured the 2-hour drive there and back would give me a chance to really find out if she was a good companion for me.

Lorraine's husband and I had gone to school back years ago, but I didn't really know Lorraine until we talked at the Captain's house.

We had a slow but steady start; a good start. We gradually did more and more things together, and we moved in together twelve months later. It wasn't a transition from one relationship to the next. My wife had gone and she wasn't coming back. It doesn't stop you having memories, but Julie-Anna wasn't 'there'. Her memory didn't intrude on my new relationship. When someone special like Lorraine comes along, you simply know and go with it.

I maintain that if you've had a good relationship, you want another one.

I believe we're meant to have company in life. Lorraine and I have now been together for 13 years.

There would have been some talk back then about it being too quick when we first got together. I met Lorraine five months after Julie-Anna died. People talk about a mandatory 12 months to grieve – that's bullshit as far as I'm concerned. Some people take a few months, some people take a few years, each to their own. I'm also well aware that others choose not to go down that path at all. It's a matter of if and when you meet the right person. I might seem superficial to some, but I'm not. What I am, is pragmatic, and determined to enjoy life.

**What do you like about your current relationship?**

This is a question I haven't considered before now, because when you're comfortable with each other, like we are, you don't look real hard at the specifics. It's when something is wrong that you look hard at things. We're comfortable. At this point in life there are no kids involved, no financial problems, none of the big triggers that cause arguments in relationships. We get on well together; enjoy doing things together. We had 28 days with seven friends on a boat in the French canals. We go overseas reasonably often. I've always had a good life, and I enjoy looking after Lorraine now. She spent 10 years looking after a husband suffering with kidney problems; she deserves a little fun now. We have a nice relationship.

**What advice would you give a friend whose spouse has died and they're having trouble getting themselves out of the house?**

I don't think there is any one answer. Grief and depression are very personal things. There is certainly no magic answer – you can't just tell someone to smile and go to a club. I would suggest they talk to some people who they can talk to easily; unburden a little. No-one can or should try to 'fix' you, but airing your thoughts helps you unravel and find your own solution. Don't expect any quick answers, but do try and overcome that lonely, depressive feeling because life has got so much to offer.

**Do you believe age gap matters?**

I have some mates who dated someone much younger than themselves, but I simply didn't want to go down that path. You would have different tastes in music, different attitudes to life in general, dear oh dear, different interests in everything! What good would I be to a 40-year-old now? I just don't believe that young and old work together – not when you're my age. That's just my opinion.

**How would you sum up your experiences to date?**

I've been extremely fortunate to have had the love of two different women, both of whom have an internal and external special beauty.

# Author's Notes

Grief is a personal journey. Don't let others rush you through it. You'll know what's right for you, and if you've lost a partner, one day you may wake up and feel that you're ready now to let someone new into your life. Since you've chosen to read *Finding Love*, you're likely feeling that that time is now or near.

Jack's words that his lost love didn't intrude on his new love, and vice versa, is a beautiful way of showing that one can love, grieve, and love again, holding both relationships sacred and unique.

## Key Points From Jack's Chapter

1. Grief and depression are very personal things. Don't let others tell you the 'rules'.
2. There may be some luck in meeting a new partner, but as the saying goes 'you make your own luck' by making intelligent decisions about who's right for you.
3. Life is brighter, fuller and more enjoyable with a best friend by your side. It is possible to fall in love again, holding both relationships sacred and unique.

# Chapter 13

## Racquel's Story

**33-years-old and suddenly a single mother with an 11-month-old baby, Racquel initially couldn't see a way forward when her marriage failed. Through ebbs, flows, a downward spiral, and a period of healing, Racquel shares what she learnt about relationships in the process of re-building.**

My first husband, Dave, and I, were together for 11 years, got married, and broke up just three years later.

We had a break from our relationship before we got married because I thought he would never marry me and never want children. I dated another man during that time. Turned out the grass wasn't greener on the other side for me. I eventually found out that the guy I was dating was still in another relationship. I was his affair. It was humiliating and my confidence took a beating. I went back to Dave after that; he was all I knew and he was safe. I tried very hard to fall in love with him again, but I don't think things were ever the same for us. I believe he never fully trusted me after our break.

Eventually Dave walked out listing all my faults and saying that he didn't love me anymore. Fourteen months later he 'came out' about his relationship with a friend of ours; part of my inner sanctum. She had looked after our baby while Dave and I went for marriage counselling. That hurt, and I couldn't help but wonder when their relationship started. There had been a night during my marriage when he went out and stayed at her place instead of coming home, and family and friends of mine had suspected that they were having an affair behind my back. I may never know the answer to that, and I no longer need to know.

For six months after Dave left I was devastated. I was grieving many things – the loss of my mother who had died 18 months beforehand, the loss of my husband, and the loss of friends. I grieved losing my ideal, happy family unit to raise my child in, and the hope of more children with my husband. The grief I felt over the family model breaking down was quite significant, and back then, to complicate matters, there was a pronounced negative perception towards single mothers. I was no longer a Wife with a capital W. Now I was a … SINGLE MOTHER with every letter a capital. It took me a while to get used to that label.

I didn't handle things well at first. I felt no hope and had an all-consuming fear of doing it 'all' on my own. I lived on cigarettes, alcohol, red wine, pot and tea. I was depressed and at various points, wanted to end my own life. I think I was manic; all highs and lows, nothing in between. This went on for six months.

I still had my close school friends, but all the friends we developed during our marriage I had met through my husband and his circle of musician friends. Some of them were initially supportive. Some dropped away immediately. Others dropped away over time because they would come over to offer me their support and I was a mess. It was a slow and gradual evolution but eventually that circle of friends all dropped away.

Dave always maintained that he was leaving me, not Max, our baby son. We shared custody of Max on a 70/30 basis with Dave having Max 30% of the time. I missed my own mother terribly during that time. I was still grieving her loss, and this grief was compounded when I had my own child and couldn't ask her for advice and tips. I thought I was doing fine, but after six months a good friend came around and told me I needed help. That day she left a business card for a kinesiologist on my table and told me to go see her. I didn't touch that card for two weeks. When I did, I commenced one of the major turning points in my life.

That poor woman had her work cut out for her the day of my first appointment! She spent two and a half hours with me. I became aware of my grief cycle, anger, resentment, hate and loathing for self. We cut some cords. Replayed things. Re-wrote some things on the screen of my life. Most importantly, I forgave Mum for dying and I forgave Dave for leaving me. They were big ones. When I later got to Dad's place to pick Max up, Dad said I looked amazing and asked for a bottle of whatever she gave me. My face had completely shifted in its exterior look.

That was the start of a newfound life. I accepted that I had to adjust to what my life was now. It had been six months; he wasn't coming back. This was my life now. I continued seeing the kinesiologist every six weeks for a few months.

I realised that the marriage break-up was not just my fault. We both made choices. My ex still blames me to this day, 12 years on, but that is none of my business. That is one of the biggest things that the kinesiologist taught me – that what my ex-husband thinks of me, or what he's doing and who he's with, are none of my business. I gradually changed my attitude and took that on.

I found freedom. Not in what I could do – you have to remember that I had a baby – but I now had inner freedom.

Dad's support had an immense impact on me. I remember calling him one night and saying, "Max's got a temperature, what do I do?" and his reply was, "I'm on my way there." Dad was always there; acting as both my Mum and Dad even though he was still grieving his wife. He definitely helped keep me grounded in reality, and his constant support was my saviour. He loved that I was seeing the kinesiologist. He's open-minded; whereas some other people around me had little time for – their words not mine – "angels and all that crap". Some people judge you no matter what you do, but Dad supported everything I did that helped me. I also saw a herbalist to even out my moods, and a woman who did a combination of massage and energy work. If you imagine your body as a tree, sometimes your roots aren't in the right soil and you get a bit off balance. I continue to use all three of these therapies to maintain a balanced and peaceful life. They are my mainstays.

Through these months of break-up and adjustment I talked to lots of friends; some were supportive, some got sick of it. I didn't stop talking. I'm a talker. It helped. But sometimes I got 'stuck'. I would be doing so well, and then I would feel like I took a huge step backwards. All these hurdles that I had to overcome kept coming up. For instance, sharing in happy milestones in friends' marriages and family life, etc.

When you separate and divorce you have to establish new guidelines because you're no longer a partner in a marriage, so that relationship has to change to a parental relationship. That's tough to work through. It's no longer about the two of you; it's now about the two of you parenting a child. It's a big adjustment.

I navigated that by constantly reminding myself that what my ex thinks of me is none of my business; I just have to do the best thing for our son all the time. Will it make Max's heart sing and will it enhance Max's life? These were the two questions I kept asking myself to make authentic decisions.

The first twelve months of being single were difficult and challenging, but then things changed. After a year, I discovered that I loved my new life, and I loved who I had become as a person. When my ex-husband had listed all my faults and blamed everything on me as he left, the things he said had embedded inside me. I believed him. For a long time I thought I was a bad person and I beat myself up constantly.

However, this led me to taking a painful, difficult and honest look at myself in the mirror. What I actually discovered was that I liked what I saw and I went through this amazing empowerment stage. I could do what I wanted and be the person who I could be. As I became happy on the inside, this projected on the outside. As a result, all my relationships improved, and my life started to change. I made a new circle of friends. I became more confident.

Falling in love with myself was wonderful and liberating. When you're feeling good about yourself, and you're starting to genuinely like yourself again, life is lighter, easier and more fun. So I started having fun. Let's face it, my ex-husband was one fish in a big ocean. Self-talk / positive affirmations are powerful. I read a lot: whether it was self-help, indulging self, or trashy novels. I started going to Noosa in Queensland with a friend for five days once a year. My ex-husband looked after Max while I went.

New friends came into my life, and some old friends started coming back. My attitude had changed. Instead of focussing on my divorce, I was now focussed on all the good things in my life: being a Mum, gardening, cooking, yoga and eating properly. It was a simple life, but a lovely life. I started to truly heal and get over my ex-husband.

The two-year mark was a turning point for me. Before then I wasn't interested in dating, but at two years, I was ready. I was no longer reacting to my ex-husband when he tried to be difficult as we negotiated over Max. I had fabulous sex with an old friend who I went to nursing college with. Perhaps I had read too many Marian Keyes novels and was vicariously living out some of her books. We had great sex for three weeks and then he wanted to move in and I was like, "Nope that's definitely not happening." That was my transition relationship. It was wonderful and freeing; I completely let go.

I continued with my kinesiologist to identify my Personal Values – a specific wish list of the traits and characteristics that I would like in my next partner. I was now visualising this person daily. I wanted to have more children; and I was excited about this person I was visualising coming into my life.

Evan was in front of me the whole time. He was my friend; I told him about every aspect of my life. He was one of the 'mutual' friends from my marriage, and the ex-husband of a friend of mine. I had known him for years. I think we met when I was about 23. He was there when Max was born. We had been through each other's relationship break-ups. He was my 'bestie' and would drop around once a week. At first he drifted on for a while when I was a mess, but he came back later.

We were sitting on my deck one day and Evan asked, "Why don't we have a casual relationship?" When I asked what he meant, he replied, "We should have sex occasionally." I told him it wouldn't work. It was too complicated. We knew each other's kids, we knew each other's ex-partners, we were best friends … way too complicated. I told him if he wanted a casual fling he needed to look elsewhere. We laughed together at what a ridiculous suggestion it was, and continued being friends; texting, calling, coffees, watching the tennis together.

Evan once offered me a shoulder rub and I was like, "Eew no … you're my best friend."

One weekend I made dinner for Evan, my Dad, and my Dad's new partner. After Evan left, Dad said to me, "Oh my God, you two are like an old married couple, just get together!"

To cut a long story short, sometimes those around us can see things we can't see ourselves. I started realising that I was attracted to Evan, I just hadn't wanted to admit it to myself because I was friends with his ex-wife. I had been so very hurt when my close friend dated my first husband and I didn't want to do the same thing to my friend now. Admittedly, my friend dated my ex immediately after we broke up, and possibly while we were still together. Evan had been separated from his ex-wife for ten years. Still … in my mind it was tricky ground.

I decided I wanted to have sex with him, so had a few wines with my sister to make sure I was relaxed, and then I called him up and invited him over. Unfortunately, I was a bit drunk and can't remember much. Evan was keen to have a relationship with me. I freaked out, and said I was sorry and that we'd made a mistake. I realised that I was now repeating a pattern. As soon as someone wanted to get into a relationship with me, I pushed them away. I acknowledged to myself that I still had a wall up and was scared of getting hurt again.

Evan and I got our friendship back on track and disregarded the sex thing. We got back into our routine of having dinner once a week and being best friends. Four months later, we spent Christmas together with Evan's son. There was nothing romantic going on. We just wanted to be in each other's company and get through the Christmas thing together. But something had changed.

We spent New Year's Eve at separate parties but spent the night texting. We missed each other. On about January 3rd I was out with some girlfriends and told them how I felt. They encouraged me to go for it, and I knew they were right. I couldn't live my life in fear of getting hurt again.

I invited Evan for a walk along the beach. That day we held each other's hand and it felt like I had arrived home. It was natural and comfortable. We went back home to my place and the rest is history. I remember kissing him and saying, "Don't ever forget this because we will never have this first kiss again." It was amazing.

**How did your friend, Evan's ex-wife, react to your new relationship?**

Badly. We both copped it from her. She called me a liar and didn't believe that we'd only just become a couple. It's interesting, nobody ever gave the friend who got with my ex straight away, a hard time. But friends of mine dumped me when I got with Evan, even though Evan and his ex had been divorced for ten years.

**What have you learnt about relationships?**

It's not so much about what I've learnt about relationships, but more about what I've learnt about myself and other people. I'm a nicer person now; more empathetic to others. Before my divorce I hadn't had any real hardship in my life. I now believe that the more hardship you have, the deeper you dig and learn about yourself. I'm truly blessed to have found the right partner now. We both liked ourselves by the time we got together. Formerly, we had both had partners who didn't make us feel good about ourselves. I'm now in a relationship where we bring the best out in each other.

**What do you believe are the essentials of a good relationship?**

1. Complete trust.
2. Communication.
3. Freedom to be yourself.
4. Freedom to express yourself.
5. Chemistry, lust, attraction. I still say to people now, ten years later, that I'm on my honeymoon. Ten years … that just sounds *crazy* but it's true.

**Do you have any advice for newly singles?**

1. Forgive yourself, and forgive your ex.
2. Take one step at a time.
3. Check in with your feelings. Recognise your feelings and write them down. Writing helps you to see your patterns of behaviour, especially if you're stuck in a rut.
4. For a woman, check in with your hormones. I think they've got a lot to answer for. I believe they're horrid, and I've suffered from them.
5. Read affirmations, self-help books, listen to songs that empower you.
6. Have belief and faith that you will get through this.
7. Have some wines with someone who makes you laugh.

8. Start to visualise your future. As much as it hurts to consider your future without them, visualise a positive future for yourself.

## Author's Notes

Reminiscent of Caroline's advice in Chapter 8 – to seek a friend intervention – sometimes those around us can see things we can't see ourselves. However, if seeking the advice of friends, choose caring, nurturing, diplomatic people who genuinely love you, and wouldn't thoughtlessly damage you through their own negativity. I can see friend interventions going horribly wrong if not handled sensitively, and wonderfully well with the right people involved.

There's a saying I subscribe to, "Before you diagnose yourself with depression or low self-esteem, first look around and make sure you are not, in fact, surrounded by assholes." A strong support network goes a long way.

# Key Points From Racquel's Chapter

1. Forgive yourself and forgive your ex.
2. Check in with your feelings and write them down. Writing helps to see your patterns of behaviour, especially if you're stuck in a rut.
3. Visualise your future. Visualisation is a proven, powerful technique that works.

# Chapter 14

## Petra's Story

**64-year-old Petra was born in Germany and emigrated to Australia with her mother in 1950. She was 3-years-old. According to the culture of the time she was verging on being an old spinster when she married at 18. Petra's story is an eloquent portrayal of changing values over time.**

I had a quiet upbringing. If there was a school dance my step-father would take me there and pick me up afterwards. It was that era when kids were restricted and very protected. Given what a no-no divorce was, it might sound unusual that I was being raised by a step-father. However, I was conceived during war to a French soldier and young Ukrainian girl. Widows *were* common back then. My Mum wasn't a widow, she and my father didn't have a chance to get married before he went away. War is cruel.

I hated my Mum at one stage. She used to say horrible things to me when I was a teenager. She once said that she wished the blood had washed me away before I was born (meaning miscarriage). I was puzzled as to why she was so verbally abusive towards me. It wasn't until I was 44 and I found my biological father, that I began to understand my Mum's behaviour.

As a 15-year-old, Mum was forcibly removed from her family in the Ukraine to work in a munitions factory in Germany. There, she fell in love with a French soldier and they conceived me. He had to go to Indo China to fight a battle and couldn't confide in her because it was a secret operation. He tried to send her back to France to live with his brother until he returned. In part because of the language barrier and in part because of her youthful naïvety, my Mum didn't understand that he was trying to protect her and that he would be gone for a long time, so she didn't go. They lost contact with each other and she came to believe that he'd been killed. She never stopped loving him.

After the war, my Mum's father told her not to return home to the Ukraine; that there were atrocious killings happening in the streets, and hunger. People were getting torn apart by being tied between two horses. Women who were thought to have slept with the enemy were being killed by having poles shoved vertically through their vaginas and up through their bodies. The country was just too unsafe, so with a 3-year-old daughter fathered to a French soldier, Mum joined the ranks of refugees trying to get out of Germany.

Chile and Argentina wouldn't accept Mum because of her illness – due to the conditions in the German factory her collarbone had rotted away. Australia would accept us, so here we are. My Mum never got over losing my Dad. Their relationship was short, but loving and beautiful – her first love.

As an adult, I wanted to learn what happened to my father. I investigated Missing Persons through the International Red Cross. It was difficult because many records were destroyed during the war. However, a copy of my birth certificate verified that my father registered me as his daughter. It took a long time, but they eventually found him. He was alive! They passed my details on to him.

When I met him, my father had a wife and new kids. He told me that my Mum was the love of his life and he'd tried three times over the years to find us. He said he never stopped thinking about us. When he married his wife she already had a 3-year-old daughter and he remembered hoping that a good man out in the world was looking after me wherever Mum and I were.

Back to my personal situation. I was 18 the first time I got married. In those days, if you weren't married by then everyone thought you were an old bag; left on the fence. Vik was the son of one of my Mum's church friends. I met him just after I left school and the first date was arranged through our parents. I was working as a clerk and sometimes Vik would pick me up for lunch. It was a treat to have a meat pie, peas, mashed potato and gravy in a café in town. At the time I thought it was all very flash.

My first dates with Vik were interesting. His mother came along to every one and would sit between the two of us. We were engaged when the first conscript for Vietnam came through. I thought I was in love. At the time I was very pleased to be getting away from my mother; she was a hard woman to live with. I was a virgin when I married, and I was embarrassed about my body and sexuality. That was the culture our parents drummed into us. Sex was a no-no. Our wedding night was a disaster. I didn't know what to do at all, and Vik had had sex once before. It hurt and I cried all night.

On our honeymoon, I got angry about my mother-in-law's interference in our relationship and marriage and there were a series of events leading up to me having an emotional outburst about it in the car. My new husband reached across and slapped me in the face – hard. I didn't talk to him for the next few days. Our marriage did not start off well.

Because we were married, Vik served his national service in Australia instead of having to go overseas. He was posted interstate so we moved and got a flat. It was a lonely time for me. I would walk to the shopping centre every day just to have something to do.

After his 2-year term of conscripted army service, we returned home, bought a block of land and built a house. We moved into our new home with our first child as a toddler. All I can recall about Vik at that time is that I had a lot of sexual urges but he didn't. Every Sunday I stayed home and did the ironing while Vik went to the club and played snooker. One Sunday there was a knock on the door – a man and a woman looking for their daughter, Jane. When I told them I didn't know anyone by that name, they said, "But she comes here every Sunday and you all go out to play snooker together." We realised that Vik and Jane were having an affair. We called it adultery in those days.

My marriage had lasted seven years and we produced two sons. It wasn't a happy marriage, but to be fair to both Vik and I, we probably were never meant for one another. We really never had a chance due to the interference from both our mothers. We were young, pressured by parents and we simply went through the motions of what was expected in our roles of husband and wife. It was a marriage of convenience.

The marriage break-up was volatile. I can only remember bits and pieces now. I went back to work and lived with my parents, and Vik had visiting access to the boys. Because of the adultery and some instances of him hitting me, our break-up was so bitter that I wouldn't let him come to the house. I used to meet him down the corner of the street with the boys. When he did have the boys he would take them to the pub and socialise with his mates and leave them sitting on the steps of the pub. That made me furious. We went through court; which wasn't nice at all, and eventually agreed that he wouldn't pay maintenance, but he wouldn't get to see the boys either.

Years later, when our oldest was 16-years-old, Vik came and saw me at work and asked to have contact with his kids. I said *okay* if the boys wished to. By then, Vik was married to a lovely lady. My boys formed a good relationship with their father and his new family. We actually all got together on occasion. Vik has since passed away, but we still get on with his wife and kids from that family.

I don't hold any grudges over my first marriage. We produced two good boys, and I think things always happen for a reason. When my first marriage ended I was around 26 years of age and financially I was in a terrible position. I had to live with my Mum and my two little boys in Mum's small house.

I met Brad through my sister and her husband. I liked him. He was fair haired, where Vik had been dark; he knew how to dance, and he had a nice body. Most important of all, he liked my boys. He had a great car, great music – Creedence Clear Water Revival – and he showed me things I didn't know. He took me out to nice places, we even saw shows in clubs. We clicked personality-wise and we loved dancing together. Vik had never taken me anywhere; I stayed home and cooked and cleaned while he went out. Brad took me everywhere. Brad was happy, athletic, vain, beautiful with blonde wavy hair, particular with his appearance, a bit of a worrier about money, and a very good worker. He accepted my boys as his own.

Back then, I never used to plan anything; I muddled my way through life. When your parents have it as tough as the parents of my generation did, you feel lucky just to be safe and have a home. You were expected to be honest, do the right thing, expect little and be happy with what you had. I thought my second marriage would be for good. I considered myself lucky that a man would take on a woman with two children.

Brad found out that the woman he thought was his sister was actually his mother, and the woman he thought was his mother was actually his grandmother. He began to agonise over this. Psychologically he never seemed to be able to handle that his real mother left him and never got him back. He felt betrayed by those closest to him. He lost confidence in himself and became a jealous and possessive person. He started drinking and went off the rails. Once he started drinking, his whole personality changed. I knew he had a drinking problem before I married him, but I convinced myself it would never become a problem. Of course I was wrong. My oldest son, Justin, was then 14 and looking very much like his father, Vik. Brad began to resent the resemblance. He started staying out late and verbally abusing Justin and me. He wouldn't let Justin's friends come to the house, and would tell Justin he was stupid. A few times I had to call the police because he was dragging me around the house. He would talk trash about me in front of the boys. One night he pulled a knife on Justin and that was it for me. I had him evicted from the house.

The worst thing I ever did, was to take him back after three months of promises of change, but once he was back in, it was on again. Within a matter of months I had him evicted again. I was a much stronger person by then. I was then 34.

I lost weight after the break-up. I was looking good – a cute, little, bubbly blonde; right at the prime of my life. However, after two disastrous marriages I vowed I wasn't going to get serious with a man for at least five years. I needed a break. I thought I'd never be able to love anyone else anyway, and I wanted to give myself time to have a bit of fun and enjoy my independence. All my girlfriends were going out on dates to restaurants, having fun here and there, and I was sitting at home alone. I got angry. I decided I was going to use men like my friends were. I was still a nice person, but I did change. I got hit on a few times, but I actually only had one 'fling' before I fell in love again. It was with this huge, Welsh man. I loved his accent and he showed me the adventurous side of life; romantic weekends away and nightclubs. He drove a red Jag. He knew how to give a girl a good time. My confidence grew, and I was doing very well at work.

I then met John at a club when I was 36, and twelve months later I knew I was experiencing something for the first time. It's hard to recognise true love until you experience it. I think that those who meet their true love the first time around and are married all their lives are very lucky.

I have now come to believe that it takes about five years to get to know someone. People are complex, but you do so much in five years that if there's something concerning there, it'll come out during that time. I don't ignore the warning signs anymore.

I kept John at arms length for about twelve months. We lived an hour and a half apart and he used to drive up twice a week just to see me for a few hours at a time. That showed me a lot. After twelve months I decided to move in with him to see if things were going to stay great or change. They stayed great and I fell deeply in love.

Over the years, John taught me just how beautiful love is. He was spontaneous and exciting. We were so compatible. If we had different opinions on something, we would respect each other's opinions. When a relationship is right, it's smooth. I think that's how you know. Everything I did, I thought of John first, and everything he did, he thought of me first. He would get up in the morning and make me a cup of tea, and if I got up first, I would make him a cup of tea. The little things count.

John and I have been together for 27 years. He's now 68. About five years ago, he started changing. I was worried that our relationship was disintegrating because he would come home from work and go to his room. It turned out that he'd had a series of small strokes. He now has dementia and he's in full-time care. I go and see him all the time. It has been traumatic to watch my big, strong, capable man enter care and not be able to look after himself. I felt so much guilt when it got too much for me to care for him at home. I hate seeing him restricted. Dementia is a cruel disease.

**What have you learnt about relationships?**

1. Beware of meddling mothers and mothers-in-law. You can't let other people interfere. You have to do what you want to do and not what other people expect you to do.
2. Sex is important. It is the connection and the happiness between two

people that creates a great sex life, and a great sex life is one of the things that keeps couples connected and strong.

3. In healthy relationships, you make your partner a stronger person, and they make you a stronger person.
4. You don't know what tomorrow will bring; make the most of your love while you've got it.

# Author's Notes

It was fascinating to interview subjects across generations. The differences in upbringing and attitudes of the times had a marked effect on their personal relationships. As Petra said, following war, she was taught to feel lucky simply to have a home and to be safe. In her second marriage, she felt "lucky" that a man would "take her on" with two kids in tow.

It took Petra three times before she felt she got "lucky" and married the right man for her. In her words, she "muddled her way through life, never planning anything."

You, on the other hand, have the benefit of knowledge and can be reflective rather than reactive to circumstances as you choose the path your life takes from this point forward.

# Key Points From Petra's Chapter

1. Don't ignore early warning signs that someone isn't right for you; that they have a Personal Value that is diametrically opposed to something very important and non-negotiable to you.
2. It takes time to get to know a person. Enjoying the lead-up and romance allows that space to know if someone's Personal Values match your own.
3. There is some luck in finding the right person, but planning and reflection heightens your chances of capitalising on that 'luck'.

# Chapter 15

## Todd's Story

**42-year-old Todd is a builder. He lives in a country town but is unfazed by the challenges this poses to dating. Although he's had long-term relationships, he's never married, and has no children … yet. Todd discusses first date and online dating etiquette.**

I had a lot to learn in my twenties and thirties. I wanted commitment and marriage, but I had five long-term girlfriends, so I've had to question myself. I knew what I was looking for – someone who I looked up to and admired – and I think self-confidence issues may have played a role in my not being with that person. I didn't have the confidence to approach girls I admired.

Now I can, but it is hard putting yourself on the line. It takes a lot of balls to walk up to someone and ask them out. Ladies, go easy on us! It's nerve-wracking; you sometimes get stuck for words or say stupid things. Please be kind to us men when that happens … (smiles), give us a chance to redeem ourselves.

I did fall heavily for one girlfriend and I thought she was the one. She had kids and we all got along well and we had a good relationship. But we broke up and got back together, and then the father of her kids moved interstate and she decided to move there too for her kids' sake. I did almost go with her; I packed my things but after a week there I knew it was too far away from my own family so we said our goodbyes and I came home.

I met my next girlfriend-to-be at the pub. I had been through heaps of upheaval and was looking for someone for companionship, and Angie was in a place in life where she'd been living at the pub and needed to get out of there. I rented her a room at my place. After a couple of years, we started seeing each other.

Our relationship was far from what I wanted. We really weren't meant for each other; we stayed together for convenience. My family didn't like her because of a few things that happened, and because she smoked dope. Eventually we had an argument and agreed we weren't happy together and broke up. We were together for five years. She'd been my best friend all that time, so it was sad, but mixed in with this was probably some fear and loneliness associated with being single at 38 years of age.

It was a reflective time for me. In my twenties I probably thought I would have a family, but suddenly I was aware that if I had kids now by the time they grew up I would be hitting my sixties. If I meet the right person, I'll probably be okay with having kids, but I also want to travel. I've only been overseas a couple of times and I'd like to do a lot more travel. Then there is the fear if I don't have kids now that later on I'll be a lonely old man and regret it. My feelings on the subject are quite mixed.

It is harder to meet people at this age than it was in my twenties but I think the key is to simply get out there. I joined a gem club – something I'm very interested in. I own an opal mine in Lightning Ridge and go there whenever I can. I did meet one girl at the gem club but it fizzled out after a few weeks.

I've put my profile on an internet dating site. That's confronting to do because you're putting yourself and your feelings online, but it is a great way of meeting people. I read a few profiles before I wrote my own and while reading I often thought, "Wow, that is something I would say about myself." Later, when I came to write my own, I wished I'd written those things down.

To be honest, I prefer to simply meet someone out and about, feel some chemistry, and take it from there, but I don't often come across single ladies with similar interests to myself. The advantage with online forums is that you know that most of the people on there are genuinely looking to meet someone. Online dating is a part of modern life. I've certainly got no interest in going to nightclubs to meet people. There comes an age when that no longer holds appeal.

I look online for people who seem to have the same interests as myself: beach, camping, rivers, someone who likes the nice things in life, but also likes roughing it in the bush. Of course looks does come into it because chemistry is an important part of a relationship, but if I saw a profile without a photo and the person's interests seemed suited to mine, I'd contact them.

A girl once contacted me and I liked her photo and she was into motorbikes and other things similar to myself. We had great chemistry on the phone, but when we met up in person, the chemistry just wasn't there. It didn't help that the photo she put online was an old one and she didn't look anything like that now. She was overweight, whereas in her online photo she wasn't.

I'm looking for a partner about the same age as myself. People say age doesn't matter, but I think it does. When you're with someone around your own age, you have similar understandings and tastes; eg. music, etc.

I've now been single for four years and I'm finding that for the first time in my life I can be happy without someone. Before I always needed someone in my life, but now I've learnt to be 'whole' on my own. Yoga has had a big effect on me in this regard. It has taken me to a place that I hadn't felt before; I'm calm and happy in the moment. My sister is a yoga teacher and for years she told me to give it a go, that it would help with my anxiety and panic attacks, and I was, "Yeah, yeah, one day". I can now say that trying and practising daily yoga is the best thing I've ever done for myself.

**How would you describe yourself?**

Fairly easy going, friendly, I can worry too much sometimes, sometimes I'm an introvert, sometimes an extrovert, loyal, twisted humour, adventurous, more of a thinker than spontaneous but sometimes spontaneous, homebody, a dreamer and a doer – it isn't often that I don't go through with something that I dream of doing.

**What do you consider good online dating etiquette?**

1. Always reply when someone contacts you, even if it's to say, "Thanks, but no thanks".
2. Post recent photos.
3. Be honest; don't play games. I don't mind if a woman I'm contacting is talking to a few people at the same time, but if they are, it's nice if they're up front about that.
4. Be genuine about what you're looking for – whether it's a relationship, a fling, commitment, or a friendship.

**First date etiquette?**

1. I don't mind paying for dinner, especially if I ask someone out. But if they ask me out, I still offer to pay. I do understand that some women don't like to feel like they owe you anything, so I don't mind when a woman wants to pay for their own meal. I'll always offer though.
2. I like to turn up on her door with a bunch of flowers, but there are creeps out there, so for the first date, especially if you've met online, it's probably best to meet at the venue.
3. Don't talk about past relationships on the first date.

**What do you think about sleeping with someone on the first date?**

I don't think it's a good idea if you're wanting to have a long-lasting relationship. Sex seems to get in the way. You get to know someone so much better when you take your time. You seem to get to know them on a different level. It's more exciting when there's a lead up, and that tends to make you value it more.

Sex on the first date can backfire for the guy too. There was one girl who I actually really liked and we were rolling drunk and it just failed miserably. When I contacted her later she didn't want to know me! *Ouch.*

**What have you learnt about relationships?**

1. There needs to be give and take and you have to have a lot of respect for each other. If you don't, things tend to go downhill fairly quickly.
2. You have to work at it. It would be great to have a relationship that was rosy all the time; but I don't think it really works that way.
3. You have to make an effort to spend quality time with each other.
4. You should do and say nice things to each other; things that come from the heart.
5. Communication must be open and honest. If issues get swept under the carpet and left unresolved, they simply build up. That's a dangerous thing in a relationship.
6. You need balance. Too much time together is no good; but so is too much time apart.
7. It's important you have similar Personal Values and interests to begin with.

**Do you feel any pressure about your age?**

Perhaps a little, but not really. Life is good at the moment. A friend of mine once told me that she wanted to be married and have a baby within two years. I found that odd, that no matter how good or bad the relationship turned out to be, she had decided she was going to have kids anyway … which she did. I think you can make a huge mistake when you think that way; you risk ending up with the wrong person.

**What would you say to a lady who says she can't find an awesome guy?**

Keep looking. We're out there (laughs).

**Do you think dating is harder for men or women?**

Surely it's got to be harder for the guys. We usually have to initiate things, and from what I've seen any time a lady does go out there are always numerous men hitting on her.

**What are your hopes for the future?**

One of my downfalls in the past has been going out with the next person who came along. It's the number one wrong thing to do! I haven't done that this time, and I'm not going to. I'm waiting until I meet that special lady who is on my wavelength, and I'm on hers.

# Author's Notes

One of Todd's downfalls in the past was going out with the first person who came along. Now he's taken the time to reflect about the Personal Values that the woman who would suit him would have, and he's gained the confidence within himself to be happy as a single man until he meets her.

Again, exercise has surfaced in another person's narrative as the means with which they became stronger within themselves. For Todd, it turned out to be practising daily yoga.

# Key Points From Todd's Chapter

1. Heal oneself before looking for a relationship.
2. Most people who register for online dating are genuinely looking for a relationship. If trying online dating, make sure you're honest in your profile and use a current photo.
3. Look for people who have similar interests and Personal Values as yourself.

# Chapter 16

## Harper's Story

**This courageous 34-year-old shares with us her thoughts and experiences as she teeters on the edge of breaking a cycle of abuse that has run through her family for three generations. I thank Harper for agreeing to be interviewed during a raw, transitional period in her life. Harper hopes that her story will help others who might be in, or coming out of, domestic violence situations.**

I was very young in my first relationship. We started dating when I was 16-years-old and had our son Geoffrey when I was 19. The relationship wasn't great and my partner was controlling. Looking back we were simply too young. He seems to have matured now in his current relationship.

My son is now 15 and he and I have an amicable relationship with his father and his new family. Geoffrey has two step-sisters through his Dad, but he doesn't feel like a part of their family. That makes me a little sad. However, I like to focus on the positives. It's good that things are amicable. I think it's important that Geoffrey has his father in his life in some capacity.

I met my second partner, Kevin, when I was 25. We met and

married within six weeks. Many will likely not find it surprising that we subsequently divorced six years later. For the first three years of my marriage, I didn't realise that Kevin was an addict. I knew he was on drugs, but he told me he was going to give them up, which he did for a while. But then he became angry and violent and I found a syringe and discovered not only was he taking drugs again, he was taking steroids as well.

Even after divorcing, we couldn't stay away from each other and continued on and off for another four years. I haven't been with anyone else since I first met Kevin, but he's had many girlfriends. We have a son and daughter together; 8-year-old Thomas and 6-year-old Rosie.

Kevin was *okay* with my first son Geoffrey, but not great. He didn't treat him like a son, and over time my son became resentful towards Kevin because of the way Kevin treated me. He was physically and emotionally abusive towards me.

I've never had a healthy relationship with a man. I've always gone for men I need to 'fix'. Now that I've acknowledged this, I've had to spend some time exploring and understanding it. In doing this, I've had to come to terms with my background.

I've reflected a lot on my upbringing to better understand myself. I was raised by my Mum, and we spent a lot of time with my uncle who was an alcoholic, and in and out of jail. We also spent a lot of time with my Nana and Grandad. I *loved* my Nana. My family was always bailing my uncle out of trouble – taking food to him when he was hiding from the police, that kind of thing. When I got older, I used to take the food to him so that my Nana didn't have to suffer through it.

I never knew who my real father was and growing up Mum used to tell me that he didn't want me. I adored one of my Mum's boyfriends but she wouldn't live with him and she told me that it was because if she let him move in he would want to touch me. My mother has always had jealousy issues towards me. I love my Mum but she is addicted to prescription medication and can be mean and erratic.

I'm addicted to food. I never want to be addicted to drugs, alcohol or medications like other members of my family because I'm well aware of what it does. My uncle recently stopped drinking and when I tell him things that used to happen, he gets angry and says I'm lying. He can't even remember the pain he's caused!

It's bizarre with my Mum. If you met her you would think she's awesome; everyone thinks she's Mother Theresa … but I know the devil inside her. Mum has said some truly horrible things to me over the years. She was mean after Nana died, and again after Grandad died. If I pull her up on things she threatens to kill herself. But I love her; I want a Mum. Doesn't everyone?

Growing up, my brothers were treated differently to me. The cycle of abuse in our family has always been directed towards women. When I had my own daughter I realised that I didn't want to continue that cycle of care/abuse that ran through our generations.

I'm still not sure who my real father is. I found out that the man I grew up thinking was my father, was not. Then I was told about two men who it could possibly be. One of them offered to have a DNA test for me so that I'd know for sure, but I no longer care to find out.

Despite all this, if you asked me if I had a great childhood, I would say "yes", because my Grandad and Nana showed me what love is.

I've been single now for a year, but to be honest, I'm still at my ex-husband's beck and call. I still take care of him and do things for him because he's on drugs. If he has no food, I let him come over and have dinner. I drive him to appointments, and I let him stay at my house when he's homeless. I'm always making sure he has food and clothes. Even though he seeks my help at times, he resents what I do for him. He blames everything that is wrong in his life on me.

During our marriage he had many affairs where he would leave me for them, and then when it didn't work out I'd have him back. I've had to do much reflection, counselling and study to understand the cycle of abuse and why I've allowed myself to remain in this cycle. I realise now that he'll never change. He's recently met someone new and now that he's occupied I'm gathering the strength to say "no" when he tries to return again.

Kevin sees himself as a good bloke and says that we belong together. He doesn't take responsibility for any of the hurt he's caused, just like my uncle. My son doesn't like Kevin because of the way Kevin treats me and to be honest if I didn't have Geoffrey I might not now have the strength to say "no" to Kevin once and for all. I'm glad that Geoffrey is giving me the strength to say "no", and I'm sad that it took me so long to do, and that I'm having to lean so heavily on my son to give myself the strength. Looking back, because I never had a dad I didn't want my kids growing up without one. I guess, in addition to that, I've never felt like I was worth more than the toxic relationships I chose for myself.

I'm working on myself. I gained weight while I was with Kevin because when I was overweight Kevin wasn't jealous, and so he was nicer to be around and didn't hit me anymore. I'm working on losing weight, and I went back to school to study a Diploma of Community Services. I've worked in aged care for 11 years, and now I want to work with disadvantaged youth. My schooling will enable me to do this. I also volunteer at a youth charity that helps teenagers with problems associated with drugs and found this therapeutic for me. When you're with an addict, you can't understand why they don't just simply give up the drugs. My volunteer work has helped me to understand the addictive personality.

I'm happy where I am right now. I acknowledge that if it wasn't for my life experiences I wouldn't have the understanding that I do. I've now done a lot of courses on drug and alcohol addiction and I understand it and am now in a position to help people through my work. When you don't have a strong functional family network yourself and a mum and dad who are present, you understand why kids get on drugs. I don't condone it, but I do understand it. I want to help these kids to know that they're important and they can make a difference and they can be a part of functioning society.

However, I've learnt that I can't help everybody. In my private life, I have to take care of myself first. I've read books to understand why people do hurtful things to others. I've also surrounded myself with a good group of friends. In the past I would always be doing more for my friends than they did for me. Now I'm more aware and take friendships more slowly. I can say "no" to people now and be okay with that, whereas in the past I wasn't able to do so. Now I take notice of the people who put just as much effort into me as I do them, and they're the ones I give myself to wholeheartedly. I've had to reconsider my whole approach to friendships and relationships.

I've now committed to myself that I will talk to a domestic violence counsellor. I've never talked about things before; I didn't feel like what was happening to me was domestic violence because I wasn't being hospitalised. Now I realise that it was and that I need to talk about it because talking aids in healing. I don't want to hold any hate in my heart.

I certainly don't look back on my life with regret because my experiences have given me knowledge and slowly but surely I'm moving forward to the next part of my life. I can feel the next part moving towards me and I know it's going to be great for me and my kids. Knowledge is power.

I love my kids so much. Now is the time … I'm breaking this cycle and my kids are going to have good influences in their lives. They're going to see healthy relationships, a healthy life, and healthy people around them. It starts with me. How are they going to respect me if I don't respect myself?

The more you talk, the more you heal. When I saw the advertisement seeking interviewees for this book I thought, "Yes, I want to speak about it and say it out loud and heal from it". Keeping it in only used to make me angry and bitter. I'm no longer a fearful person. I read a positive affirmation every day now. I'll never be in a toxic relationship again. I'm happy on my own with my kids. I'm finding myself, losing weight, pursuing my career, and happy to wait for the right time and the right man before entering another relationship.

**What have you learnt about relationships?**

1. If it's not a healthy relationship, especially if there is domestic abuse, get out straight away. If other people are telling you it's not healthy; listen to them.
2. If your partner makes you cry more than they make you happy, then it's not okay.
3. Be true to yourself. If your partner puts you down and says you can't do something, then that isn't a healthy relationship. In a healthy relationship, partners support and encourage each other, not hold each other down.

# Author's Notes

One in three Australian women will be affected by domestic violence in their lifetime and I don't think any woman thinks they will become an addition to that statistic.

More and more women, including famous personalities such as Mariah Carey, are now speaking out about being victims of domestic violence and this is a good thing in terms of tackling an endemic community problem. In the March 2014 issue of Australian *Women's Weekly*, actress Rachael Taylor, said, "At first, my reasons for keeping my experience of domestic violence to myself were very simple. I felt ashamed. I felt stupid. I felt very sad. And there was another reason. Domestic Violence is not very nice to talk about. Not for the survivor of it, nor the community at large."

Rachael went on to explain that she ignored early warning signs because she didn't think she was the "type" of girl to fall victim to domestic violence.

"My life got very small. To me, it felt like my entire social network had shrunk to the number of one and one-quarter of a person. It was as if one whole person was allocated for my abuser and the other quarter was me. I'm not sure where that three-quarters of me went exactly," she said.

If you, a friend or a family member are experiencing or have experienced domestic violence, I encourage you to reach out to the support that is available. www.whiteribbon.org.au has a list of all the Australian national and state helplines. Reaching out will make a difference.

# Key Points From Harper's Chapter

1. Victims of domestic violence sometimes talk themselves into believing that what is happening to them is not actually domestic violence.
2. Reach out to organisations like White Ribbon for support, advice and information. There is knowledgeable help available. Talking to trained counsellors aids healing.
3. Isolating yourself can keep you vulnerable to your abuser.

# Chapter 17

## Bernie's Story

**Bernie was lonely when his wife left, but he also came to enjoy himself. His marriage break-up paved the way for a woman perfectly suited to him to enter his life, and the lives of his children. Now enjoying retirement, Bernie provides practical insights on combining two families.**

My first marriage lasted from 1974 – 1987 and we dated for 18 months before getting married. I was 21-years-old when I became a husband. We had two children together – Joanie (now 38) and Anton (36).

Our marriage was a new, exciting phase in life. We both saw it as a way to leave home and start an adventure, which seems fairly immature now. We had nothing, only a couple of hundred dollars in the bank. Together we built things up.

About six or seven years into our marriage, I think Roxanne thought, having wed so young, that she'd not enjoyed life. Towards the end I don't think she particularly even liked me anymore.

After Roxanne left, the kids lived with me and stayed with their Mum every second weekend.

I was shattered, and lonely. I guess I knew during my marriage that she wouldn't be around forever, but I ignored the feeling. I probably wasn't a confident person to start with, and this knocked my confidence around more. I had two kids to look after, so I didn't have a lot of time to think about the future or to wallow in self-pity. I had to look after the kids, get them to school, manage our day-to-day lives, do all the house cleaning, etc

Whilst I was hurting deeply, I knew that I never wanted to patch it up with her. I resigned myself to the fact that my marriage was over, and made a conscious decision to get on with life, look after the kids, and see what would come of it all.

There was one bonus to my new life, I now enjoyed having every second weekend all to myself. After getting married so young, this was entirely new to me. I went fishing, and had a group of guys who I'd meet up with for a beer on Saturday afternoons. After a while I started quite enjoying these aspects of it. But I was lonely.

I was single for a few years. I always knew that I wanted another relationship, but I wasn't actively looking for one. I believed that in the natural course of being out and about I would simply one day meet someone, we would click, and it would go from there.

I met Natalie when our boys started playing football together. We already knew each other, and I knew that her husband had died at around the same time that Roxanne left me. Over the years we'd seen each other around; Natalie lived about five streets away from me. Our kids were all very close in age and played together.

Natalie knocked on my door one day and asked if I'd like to go out with her and some friends; a date with a group of people. I said "yes", so long as she would come with me to my brother's 40th birthday party. Natalie is good company. We went out to the Italian restaurant down town. Even now, we're still friends with the people who we went out with that night. Our relationship progressed slowly but surely. We were both preoccupied and busy looking after kids. Over time, we came to spend more time together.

Natalie and I got more and more comfortable with each other. We're both easy going and make each other laugh a lot. She had a holiday caravan at a beach side location and we'd spend some time down there; both families together. It felt right. I was happy. I could tell Natalie anything and everything, and the four kids kept us busy.

I proposed to Natalie just before her 40th birthday and we announced it at her birthday party. Following that, Natalie put her house on the market and it sold quickly. There we were with two lots of furniture, us, and four kids in a 3-bedroom cottage. We put wardrobes down each of the rooms to give each kid their own space. Four kids with four different personalities! Kids who were each used to having their own rooms.

Natalie had received advice to avoid waiting to progress our relationship until the kids all moved out of home. Having now been through it myself, I do believe it's worth being together and working through the issues with the kids. We immediately commenced renovating to put an extension on the house.

It was difficult for Natalie's kids – their father had died. It wasn't just about moving house, it was about leaving the memories of their father. Timmy (Natalie's son) was angry for a while. And whilst my daughter, Joannie, and Natalie's daughter, Kylie, were at school together, becoming step-sisters is a very different kettle of fish. We had one bathroom – that was a of a bit nightmare! We had all the normal teenage issues, times four.

**What makes your relationship with Natalie work?**

Honesty and friendship. Natalie is my best friend. We like similar things, I care for her and she cares for me. We've had some great holidays and road trips. I'm probably not as good a communicator as I should be. Sometimes it takes me a while to speak up; I fall back into being not as confident as I should be. But usually our communication is good.

If our relationship wasn't right, the kids would have sensed it, but the kids knew – we were, and are, good for each other.

**After all these years how do you keep your relationship strong?**

We like going away for four or five days by ourselves, and now that we're both retired, we can. We take the caravan down to the bay or somewhere like that. We also like simply going over to the local club and having a few drinks together. Conversation is never difficult.

**Why do some relationships work and some don't? Is there a secret formula?**

No. There's luck in finding the right person, but having said that, you make your own luck. Each relationship is different. Also, relationships can be pulled apart by other factors than the two people themselves. For instance, families can play a big part in the success of a relationship.

Natalie and I respect each other's alone time. I like trekking and sometimes go away for 2-week remote trekking adventures with a group of friends – men and women. You do need a bit of time to yourself in a relationship. That is one of the tests in retirement – allowing the other person to have a bit of time to themselves. Time apart is good because it adds variety to your life, provides input into the relationship – new subjects for discussion when you return home. I play golf every Tuesday and Natalie has coffee with the girls so when we get back together there's stimulation around that.

**What have you learnt about relationships?**

1. They should never be taken for granted. You can have the happiest marriage in the world, but you just never know what might happen. You have to continue to work on your friendship together and not hold grudges so that you can get through anything that might come your way.
2. Jealousy is a curse. Natalie hasn't got a jealous bone in her body. She could have been jealous because I've had some very strong friendships with women I've worked with – all platonic, they're just nice people with common interests. Rather than being jealous, Natalie became friends with them too. Jealousy puts a wedge in relationships, and then you start missing out on things. For instance, if Natalie was

jealous, I would have missed out on some of the amazing treks I've been on. Honesty and trustworthiness are probably Natalie's best attributes.

3. You have to be faithful. If you commit to a relationship, commit to it. If you're going to fool around, finish your relationship first because it mustn't be the right relationship for you. By your actions, your partner knows if they can trust you.

**What are your tips for handling a sudden break-up?**

1. Always look for the positive. Your life might have changed, but it's changed for a reason. In hindsight, you'll look back and see there were problems and a reason why it had to change.
2. Look to the future, not the past.
3. Don't grieve too long or you'll risk becoming bitter, and bitterness is no good for anybody.
4. If a relationship ends it's very difficult to remain friends. Let them go and move on.
5. A break-up is a chance to reinvent yourself, and with a bit of maturity in you now, you're more aware of who you are. But don't ever lose the kid in you – you have to have fun.
6. Above all, be positive. Your new life could turn out to be way better than your old one; that's what happened to me.

**How do you think single people should meet other single people?**

1. You'll not meet people sitting at home looking at four walls. You need to get out, but don't force the issue, it'll happen. Don't panic; don't press it too hard. It *will* happen. Join an organisation like Table Talk where there's no pressure. You just go out to dinner and meet other single people.
2. I'm not a fan of meeting people online. I suggest joining groups about things that you're interested in. You'll meet people and you'll have common interests to discuss. Natalie and I both love having BBQs and that is basically how we first met – going out with friends.

**As you mentioned earlier, sometimes confidence takes a beating after a break-up. How do you repair that?**

Talk to your friends or talk to a professional. Admit to someone that you're doing it tough, and if they're friends they will help you out. There is no shame in it.

**Did you find it difficult losing friends after your marriage failed?**

The loss of mutual friends following a break-up can be difficult. Friendships change; just accept it. It's natural and normal. I'm 60-years-old now and when I look back I can see that I've had different friends for different chapters in my life anyway.

**How have friends / family members affected yours and Natalie's marriage?**

Family relationships are important, but they're not the be all and end all. The most important people in a relationship are you and your partner. Families can be difficult – there can be problems. You have to support each other in relationships with family. You have to present to both families as a unit.

I say to people now, "If a friend of yours has had a divorce or separation through death, accept their new partner – it'll go a long way towards helping their relationship. It can be tough being the new man or woman."

**What are the warning indicators that someone isn't right for you?**

1. Interests are different, and there's no tolerance for the differences.
2. You start to do things separately without asking each other to go.
3. You're uncomfortable with the way they behave. For example, flirtations, too much drinking. If you don't address those issues they can become a burr in the saddle.

**What are the keys to a happy relationship?**

1. The most important thing in a relationship is friendship because friendship is usually built on aligned Personal Values, interests, acceptance, honesty, respect, openness, a bit of admiration for the

other person, understanding. A long-term friendship is similar to a long-term relationship. You understand that people can't always be bubbly and happy, sometimes they're going to be down and want to kick the cat.

2. If a relationship builds slowly it's more likely to be genuine.
3. A good relationship builds a solid family. We managed to bring four kids together – they're now all 38 and 36, they've all got kids of their own. I think that is a big credit to Natalie and a great achievement. My son had his step-brother as his best man at his wedding. I'm very proud of that.
4. Share the responsibilities – don't leave it all up to one.

I have to say, it is a hell of a lot easier to talk in hindsight. It would have been difficult to see things this clearly at the time of my break-up.

## Author's Notes

Focussing on the positives and the future, as Bernie did, is one of the keys to success in creating your ideal future. As Bernie said, you make your own luck. Get yourself 'out there' with a positive attitude, and you'll find like-minded people are attracted to you in return. This can be easier said than done. The Self-Reflection Exercises in Section 3 will help you achieve this.

## Key Points From Bernie's Chapter

1. If you've just experienced a break-up, your life might have changed, but it's changed for a reason. Looking back, you'll see there were problems and a reason why it had to change.
2. Be positive. Your new life could turn out to be way better than your old one.
3. A break-up is a chance to reinvent yourself; a chance to reflect, learn, grow and create something new, positive, simply divine. Take control of your future by making good decisions for you.

# Chapter 18

## Natalie's Story

**Natalie tragically lost her first husband quite young. His death left her alone with two children. She shares her grief, and how, later, she met and fell in love with Bernie (from previous chapter).**

I married my husband, Karl, when I was 20-years-old. We'd been married 17 years and had two young children together, when Karl had a heart attack at 39 years of age.

I was absolutely in love with him and we had an excellent marriage. He was a truck driver when we met and later a shift worker at a smelter works; a bit of a rough and tumble type person. He was manly, outdoors-ish, a boxer. We had a good sex life, and loved socialising together with friends.

He was at work at the smelter when he felt a pain down his arm and he thought he must have been poisoned by gas or something. He had a high pain threshold so he battled on through the afternoon, and then a friend drove him home. When he arrived home, he stumbled a bit. I knew he must have been in a lot of pain when he asked me to call the doctor. The pain was across his arm and upper chest, not his heart. He described it as like a bad indigestion.

The doctor came to the house and told him he might be having a heart attack. He was given a tablet to put under his tongue, and when that relieved the pain, it confirmed to the doctor that it was, indeed, a heart attack. An ambulance took him to hospital. After a couple of days they said he was okay and sent him back to work. They gave us tablets that he needed to take if he experienced any more pain.

He gave up smoking, and took up walking. We modified our diet.

About six weeks later, we were at his sister's place, swimming in her pool, when he experienced a huge pain while Kylie, our daughter, was on his shoulders in the pool. We had forgotten to take his tablets with us, so we hurried home to get them. He was screaming in pain by the time we got there. He asked me to call an ambulance, and they again took him to hospital. I got dressed, had a shower, and then met him at the hospital.

They waited for him to stabilise, and then drove him slowly to a bigger hospital. We saw a cardiologist and he told us that Karl wasn't going to pull through. I was in shock, scared. We were told he had 24 hours to live. How were the kids going to survive this?

Three weeks later he was still in hospital, conscious, and they had a line on him to read his heart. They eventually moved him out of coronary care and up to a ward. I thought he was going to be fine. Karl was feeling quite positive, but then they told him he needed a heart transplant to stay alive. He didn't handle that news very well. A few days later a social worker requested to see me, and she asked if Karl had explained to me that it was unlikely that he was going to make it. He hadn't. That shocked me because I thought he was getting better.

On 22 December, the hospital called me and said I should come in, that he'd had another turn. I was devastated, thinking, "Oh no, we're back to the beginning again after he'd come so far." I called my sister-in-law and we drove to the hospital together. When we got there, instead of seeing him with all the lines back in him again, the staff were waiting for me and told me that he'd died. They hadn't wanted to tell me on the phone. He'd had another heart attack and they tried to revive him but couldn't. Sadly, at the time he died, his parents were in the waiting room, waiting to see him.

The staff asked if I wanted to see him. I wasn't sure. His sister didn't want to go in, and I didn't want to go in alone. In hindsight, now, I wish I had. He had his first heart attack on the 3rd October, and we had his funeral on Christmas Eve.

Our son, Timmy, was 10, and our daughter, Kylie, was 13.

When I told Kylie that her father had died, she kicked and cried, but when I told Timmy he just stared at me and said, "Can I go back out and play now?" It took him three years to cry over his father's death. I didn't experience the effects of Karl's death immediately either. I had to be the strong one. My daughter was stressed, my Mum was in hospital, my sister had a mental illness and was out of control at the time. I went about informing people, and making the necessary arrangements. It was a few days after the funeral that it all hit me.

We had a caravan for weekends at the beach. My friends were down there, so I took my kids there for most of January, through the school holidays. That trip helped us all.

I didn't cry in front of the kids, which in hindsight wasn't a good thing. I talked to Kylie about that years later. She said she would have liked to see me cry. At the time I thought I was doing the right thing for the kids. I cried each night when I went to bed. I went to the doctor and got some sleeping tablets. I took them for a short time, but not long, because I didn't want to get addicted. After a period of months, I took one every second night but the nights on which I didn't take one I got very little sleep. I probably weaned myself off them over a period of 12 months. It was so long ago now that it's difficult to remember the exact details. Certainly the grief was long and painful.

I missed him dearly – the security of having him there, the family bond, his love and friendship, and him doing things with the kids. He was very handy; he could put his hand to anything, and now I had to do everything alone. The kids were probably my saviour. You think about the kids more than yourself because they need you to look after them – it's simply human nature.

I grieved for at least 12 months. The first anniversary of his death was very difficult. I was desperately missing him; sad and lonely, especially after the kids went to bed. I leaned on my friends a little, but I didn't like to impose.

Going to BBQs as a single mother was hard. Friends would invite me over, which was nice, but they were an affectionate couple – always holding hands or him putting his arm around her. That would privately upset me.

It was 15 months after Karl died that I asked Bernie out. I felt a little bit of guilt, but I was only looking for friendship when I first asked him out. I simply didn't want to go to BBQs on my own anymore. Our children were friends. I knew Bernie through our boys playing football together – it wasn't as if he was a stranger. I think if Bernie had been a stranger, Timmy wouldn't have accepted it at all. We initially saw each other about once a fortnight, and as our friendship grew we saw each other more often.

I was missing my husband, but I didn't want to let it on to Bernie unless he asked me. I found Bernie to be such a lovely person.

This was all a long time ago now; 1987 to be precise.

One day a police car pulled up outside and out got Timmy. He'd been playing on the railway line with Bernie's son and some other friends. Timmy got out of the police car, pale as anything. I was so cranky, and gave him a hell of a blast. I was so upset, and I was angry at Karl that he was no longer there and I had to handle it on my own.

Falling in love with someone else, is obviously poignant. I had to get used to Bernie's ways – he was very different from Karl. Bernie, though, is so very gentle, that his nature probably made things easier for me to adjust to. Probably the hardest part for me was six months into it, when Bernie and I slept together for the first time. That was confronting, but I knew it was time to move on. I was not in a rush to get married again though.

Bernie was sensitive towards the fact my husband had died. His break-up was a divorce. Divorce and death are quite different situations. At the time Karl died, Bernie and his wife had come to my house together to tell me that they were splitting up just a few days after Karl passed away. We all knew each other but they hadn't heard about Karl yet.

Bernie and I married four years later.

**How did you know that Bernie was right for you?**

I don't think you ever know 100%. Certainly, things like the way he treated me – like a queen. He's fallen down a little bit in that area since then actually! When I first met him, he would always open the door for me, etc. As I'm talking I'm realising the little bugger doesn't do that anymore.

Also, I liked his sense of humour. We have slightly different senses of humour, and we make each other laugh often.

**What makes your relationship with Bernie work?**

1. Trust.
2. I'm happy for him to do things without me.
3. Similar interests.
4. Communication – we always talk things through. We don't really seem to have any issues now.

**Having now interviewed yourself and Bernie, you both seem more casual and at peace with commitment than others I've talked to. Why do you think this is so?**

I think it was the era we were born in – the 1950s. You could walk up the main street at any time of the day or night without feeling threatened. Life was all about music, dance, simple fun. It was a straightforward era that carried through in our personalities. All of my friends who were born in the same era, think the same as we do – we simply go out and enjoy life. We like life to be simple.

**What's next for you and Bernie?**

Travel, and spending time enjoying our family and friends.

**What advice would you give to a single friend who is lonely and struggling after the death of a spouse?**

1. Stay busy with things you're interested in – dancing, sport, movies – keep busy and life follows. If she's got children at home, I think there is more opportunity out there now for a woman to get involved in certain things and still be with her children; eg. sport.
2. It has to be someone very special to fall in love again, but really, that's probably a good thing.

# Author's Notes

Grief is a very personal journey and no-one else should tell you how long and in what way to grieve. You'll know what's right for you. Talk to good friends and/or counsellors or health professionals when and if you need to, especially if you feel that you're 'stuck'.

Since you're reading this book you're most likely ready, or very near, to letting someone new into your life and into your heart. Take comfort in knowing that others have successfully had two distinct love relationships where both partners were special and treasured.

## Key Points From Natalie's Chapter

1. Stay busy with things you're interested in.
2. It has to be someone very special to fall in love again, and that's a good thing.
3. Falling in love again is possible with sensitivity on both sides.

# Chapter 19

## Gemma's Story

**Gemma married young when she fell unexpectedly pregnant. She shares why this marriage later failed, and the different approach she took choosing her second partner to ensure her next relationship would be an enduring one.**

I was in Grade 12 at school when I met my first husband, Jim. He was the older brother of a girl at school and we'd been dating for a year when I discovered I was pregnant. My Mum gave me two options. I could either get married, or she would stick me in a home for the duration of the pregnancy and then I would give the child up for adoption before returning home. If I chose the second option, I wasn't allowed to ever see Jim again. Jim and I got married. I had my daughter, Stacey, shortly after my nineteenth birthday.

Jim was a regular drinker, and I was a social drinker and non-smoker. We sort of lived separate lives because we had very little in common. He wondered why I couldn't simply relax and have a drink. For my part, his drinking stressed me out. I found that everything had a consequence. For instance, if I needed him to do something like look after the kids or come with us to a family thing, he would only do so on the condition that in return he later got to go to the pub and get drunk with his mates.

I felt like I shouldered most things alone. I worked full-time and raised two daughters. Jim was right. I was stressed! Largely because we just weren't suited to each other. I was finding life difficult and tiring.

It wasn't me who broke off the relationship in the end. When he left me, Jim contacted my mother, father, cousins and friends and told them that he still loved me but that he couldn't live with me because of the way that I was. I had a lot of relatives saying to me, "What's wrong with you?" and "Get yourself fixed," and "Why won't you take him back?" I was lucky to have a couple of girlfriends who took turns phoning me every day – they were always there for me if I wanted to talk. I was bitterly disappointed by the people who took his word for it without asking me for my opinion, but I never had it out with them. Outside, I held it together, but inside I was crumbling. It was very tough.

My daughters were 17 and 14 when my marriage ended. When he first left, Jim didn't contact the girls. Before the split, he was the good cop and I was the bad cop, so the girls desperately missed their Dad. Within a couple of weeks of the break-up, I had a disagreement with Stacey and she phoned her Dad and got him to pick her up. She moved in with her father and grandfather, but she soon realised that on weekends her father wasn't there, and there was no-one to drive her around to friends or the library. After six weeks she moved back in with me.

I was devastated to find myself single at 36 years of age. At first I thought Jim would come back. I went to a counsellor, and got Jim to go to the same one. He went to one session, and the counsellor then told me that Jim wasn't coming back.

Six months later we all found out he was living with another woman and that he'd been having an affair on me, so all those people who blamed me ended up finding out the truth eventually. Once I discovered he had a new woman, my thinking shifted and I started looking after myself. I threw myself into my work and further developed my good reputation there. Feeling good at work was good for my self-esteem.

The following year (18 months after our separation), I went on a cruise with five of my female cousins and friends. We were all looking for love for the second time around on that cruise, but we ended up on a country and western cruise. Not my scene at all – so no love for me, but I did have a good time.

I returned home from that cruise, happy within myself and ready for someone new to come along. I didn't go out actively looking, but nor did I sit at home anymore. I accepted every invitation that came my way. I have a big extended family and we socialise together a lot so the invitations mostly came from family, but there were always new people from outside family at every gathering.

Then a cousin met a guy at her friend's baby's christening. He had split from his wife 12 months earlier and they both thought that he and I would be suited. Like me, he came from a great family. She asked if she could give him my number and I agreed. I thought that even if I made a new friend to go to movies with, that would be nice.

When he called we talked for an hour and a half and I thought he seemed nice. He asked me to dinner and a movie the following Friday night. My first husband, Jim, was six foot one, built like a brick s^&t house, and overly confident – definitely an air of FIGJAM (F%^& I'm good just ask me) about him. When I answered the door to Michael, he was the same height and weight as me. There was nothing of him! I thought, "Where's the rest of him?"

He took me to dinner. He hardly ate anything so neither did I because I didn't want to look like a guts. Following that we went to a terrible movie but the movie didn't matter as we had a great time. Next, he came to a family gathering at my place for my birthday. My sister was most impressed with him. Our third date was to see the great movie *Last of the Mohicans* and then he took me to Jimmy's on the Mall in Brisbane and we sat near the heater and had a late dinner. I decided then and there that he was mine.

Michael doted on me. I had never had that before. Having had kids so young, Jim and I could never afford much, and here was this guy buying me flowers, chocolates and wine, and taking me to dinners and movies every weekend. My daughters were worried that I only liked him because he bought me things. They found it difficult to accept me having a new man in my life. His kids also found it difficult to accept me into their father's life and they weren't friendly towards me. I now have a good relationship with some of his kids, but not all of them.

Michael and I remained 'dating' for five years because of the kids' ages, and because we both had very different styles of raising our kids. We got engaged and lived together after most of our kids had left home; we only had my youngest and his youngest living with us.

Michael and I got through those early years by understanding that we had to be a 'unit' in front of the kids. Our relationship is supportive. We know each other's negatives but we are still there for one another. For instance, when one is down the other will lift them. We're comfortable with each other. We have had some major health issues and been there for each another. He's had depression and we worked through that together, and I had a serious car accident that has led to years of rehabilitation and he's been there for me. We have the same interests, and we like the same things. We started our relationship with mutual problems with our exes. Both of them left each of us, leaving us devastated, so we had that common thing to start and this continued to progress into other common interests. A couple of months down the track when our relationship became physical *Oh My God* it was good, and still is.

Before I came into his life, Michael thought that a mother shouldn't work. But as you do, you learn from each other in a new relationship. I have always worked, and now Michael can see the benefit of that. We have modest jobs, but when we're both working we have more money to do all the things we like doing. We live off his wage, but the more I earn, the more we can travel, and we like that. We're heading to Bali for the fifth time in a couple of months.

**What have you learnt about relationships?**

1. You have to be yourself. You have got to be happy and love yourself the way you are – warts and all – before someone else can come along and love all of you.
2. Mutual interests are important, and some mutual goals. Michael and I know what our team goals are: to be comfortable in life, to enjoy our kids and grandkids, and to travel for as long as we can.
3. I believe that you need to have sex at least once a week to maintain a healthy relationship. It should be spontaneous, not pre-planned. When you're with the right person, everything is just easy. I didn't have a good sex life with my first husband, but Michael takes me to heaven and back. Neither of us are perfect, but we find each other's bodies very sexy. I want to be 90-years-old and still doing it. Mutual interests and a great sex life keep snowballing into better and better things.

**What would you say to someone who is broken hearted?**

Don't rush it; don't go looking. Give yourself time to mend your broken heart. Do things that make you happy; actively pursue your interests. Also, never say "no" to any reasonable invitation, even if it is couples inviting you out. Go out simply to relax and have a good time with people – that will lead to you loving yourself more, and the right person will come along in good time.

**How do you think single people should meet other singles?**

Through family if you are lucky enough to have a big, social family like I do. Otherwise, join interest groups. For example, I would have joined a social tennis group, or Parents Without Partners.

**What is the key to good communication?**

Talk about *everything* with your partner. I used to keep things bottled up when I was with my first husband and then something would make me really angry and I would just explode out of the blue. It doesn't work. He used to call me "looney" because I would explode at something little – like the beds not being made – but he never realised that I was exploding about two months worth of built-up frustrations. And to be fair to him, how could he?

Michael and I talk about stuff as it's happening. It doesn't matter if we don't agree, but it is important that everything's out in the open and we both know how the other feels about things.

**What would you say are the top five things you have learnt about relationships?**

1. Be yourself.
2. When it's right, it's easy. You're free of inhibitions and free to express yourself without critical judgement.
3. You need to talk about everything as it happens. There are always things to learn from each other, and open communication allows that to happen.
4. It's important to take time and enjoy each other's company. Don't let the pressures of life take over. You must make sure there is always time in every day to spend time with each other.
5. When you disagree on a big issue, see a counsellor together. A third party gives an impartial perspective; they give you the tools and suggestions to reach a healthy compromise together.

**What advice would you give to a single friend who is struggling?**

1. Talk, talk, talk to all who care and want to listen. Have your support network around you. Sometimes, you might only want to talk for five minutes, sometimes you need to talk for hours.
2. Take time for yourself and do things that make you happy.
3. Keep yourself busy so you don't just sit and mope.
4. Take your time choosing a new partner to make sure you make a good choice.

# Author's Notes

Combining families is complex. There are many personalities, perspectives and needs that must be accommodated. It takes sensitivity, understanding, patience, communication and goodwill by all parties – and obviously this can be tricky. The intricacies of blending families to ensure all members can live happily in the new dynamic is a topic too great to be thoroughly explored in this book. However, there are many good books, counsellors and mentors available to assist and guide if needed. Blending families could possibly be one of the greatest tests of open communication principles with so many differing people and challenging dynamics to consider and accommodate. The rewards of success, however, are worth it.

# Key Points From Gemma's Chapter

1. Accept every reasonable invitation to socialise that comes your way. This is a common theme that came through in the interviews. Interviewees' expressed that new opportunities, positive energy, enthusiasm and laughter came their way most times they made the effort to socialise, even on days they initially didn't feel like going out.
2. Take time choosing a new partner to ensure you make a good choice. The person you choose is ideally going to be in your life for years to come. Don't under-value the importance of the choice you're about to make.
3. Personal Values don't all have to be the same, but critical Personal Values must align, and there must be mutual respect and acceptance of negotiable Personal Values. Differing Personal Values regarding alcohol consumption, socialising with friends and child raising were serious problems that became insurmountable in Gemma's first marriage.

# Chapter 20

## Robyn's Story

**60-year-old Robyn is in her third marriage. She's learnt much. Her story covers many countries and many adventures.**

Things were different in Jamaica. I was 17-years-old, impressionable, went to an all-girls school in England, and met a young man about town with a lot of cash. I was seduced by all the stupid stuff like being able to go out to lovely places and drink champagne. He was six years older than me, and married. That was somewhat irrelevant at that time and in that place. It was quite the done thing over there. Back then, Jamaica was a macho society and most of the men had mistresses.

However, I always believed I was going to be the wife, not just the mistress. A wedding was the goalpost for me to prove to all the naysayers around me that he was, indeed, going to marry me. I was determined to prove that I was different to all the others and that he did love me. The clandestine nature of the relationship probably added to the excitement for me. My parents were absolutely against it.

He eventually got a divorce and moved in with me when I was 21. We got married when I was 26. My parents didn't come to the wedding.

After we married I was like, "Oh, is this all it is?" He started talking about us having children and I was thinking, "No, not with you." That was a wake-up call for me that this was not the relationship of my life after all and perhaps I should be doing something else. I also started to realise that given that he'd had an affair on his first wife, he would probably end up doing the same to me. I was 28 when I left him.

I then got a great job with Air Florida. There was little responsibility, no taking work home. The girls I worked with were quite wild; I was staid compared to them. They often shocked me with their wildness. They were great times. Some friends of mine who were launching a squash and racquetball club in Fort Lauderdale, Florida said they had a friend that I absolutely had to meet. We all had a night out at a lovely restaurant / wine place. The guy they introduced me to was English like me, and a broker at a big investment firm. The first thing that attracted me to him was sharing the same culture. I had lived out of England for about 10 years by that time so it was great fun to talk to someone about Cadbury's chocolate and Dr Who and all those shared background topics. Our first lunch date went on for hours talking about all those things we both missed. He was vivacious and had a strong character about him. I told my flatmate, after just a couple of dates, that I felt I was going to marry him. Two years later, I did.

Our relationship was tumultuous. Although he came from a good family in Dorset, he had already squandered a fortune by the time he was 21. That should have been a warning signal for me, but somehow I managed to gloss over that. He always wanted the big things. He was never happy with earning simply good money, it always had to be *big* money. We had two adorable children together; girls. We moved to Texas where he got into precious metals and then oil wells. He invested big money, and lost big money. When he lost everything I discovered that he'd also lost all our savings that we had left in a bank account in England.

Money didn't matter so much to me. Even though earlier I said I was seduced by money, it's actually not a big driver for me. Personally, I live quite frugally. Ultimately it was his drinking that drove us apart. I was scared sometimes to leave the girls in his care, and his drinking started causing friction with our friends. I couldn't cope with it and took the girls back to England. I told him he could come with us if he wanted, but he didn't. The girls were 7 and 5 at the time.

Thus, in 1991, I was a 39-year-old single woman raising my two girls alone. I moved to a small village location in England. It was difficult to develop relationships. There were no groups of single mothers in small village locations, and the stigma back then was that I must be a loose woman because I no longer had my husband with me. So the women didn't accept me easily, and of course, developing friendships with men was difficult because the women saw me as a threat.

I eventually dated a veterinarian for five years. Again, he was older than me. He was a commitment-phobe and since he was a locum vet he would often travel. Everything in our relationship was on his terms. Sometimes, he would come home for a weekend after being away for weeks, and he would only stay part of the time and leave. I blame his mother. She used to say to him all the time, "You're such a disappointment to me John." He was a great vet, and a great artist, but he'd never been in a live-in relationship. He did say at one stage that I was the love of his life, and we rented a house together, but he never moved in!

Luckily I had just finished my teaching degree so I was self-sufficient. I bought a house and my girls and I moved into it.

I believe that when you're a single man, you're always invited to things. But it's the opposite when you're a single woman because other women see you as a threat. Plus, the kind of things I liked doing – dancing, writing courses, teaching – were probably not conducive to meeting men. They were all female dominated pursuits. I was introduced to my next partner, Tony, through friends, and I wanted someone to go out with so we dated for about three years. My relationship with Tony was quite good, but again, I did feel like it was all on his terms. He was quite set in his ways, and I felt like I had to fit in around him, rather than him fitting into my life.  My Dad got sick and I wanted to move to Australia to be close to my family who had all moved there a few years beforehand. When I moved to Australia, Tony didn't want to come, so that was the end of that.

Arriving in Australia I was 49-years-old. My younger daughter, Lilly-Rose, was at high school and I met a couple of women through her friends at school. My social network grew from there. One particular couple I befriended had met on an online dating site. I decided online dating was actually quite a good way of screening people. If they couldn't spell I wouldn't give them a second chance. My daughter took my photo and helped with my profile. It was quite surprising; I immediately started talking to a few interesting men. I met a couple of them for coffee and had a few laughs but nothing more. One of them in particular was quite nice and seemed suited to me – a university professor – but you just know when you meet someone if *its* there or not. Another one was crying into his coffee while we were talking so it was quite obvious that he wasn't ready for a relationship.

I started seeing one gentleman. He was politically green, interesting, and organised fascinating road trips. I enjoyed his company. He started wanting a more serious relationship, but I didn't. The spark just wasn't there, plus he was still living with his ex-wife.

Then I met Hugh on the internet site. He was quite short on the email, and I'm a writer so I preferred lengthy writing. But Hugh was like, "Well, enough of this, let's meet up, no point continuing to write if we don't hit it off in person." We met, and we hit it off.

He proposed to me in a beautifully romantic way. We were walking on a high hill at Coomba Park, and he proposed 'properly'. I wasn't expecting it. It was lovely.

We've now been together for 10 years.

**What makes your relationship work?**

We're simply really happy together. We share the same Personal Values; the same ideas about community and environment. Obviously, we've got different opinions on some things, but our lifestyles are similar. We're not big 'things' people; we don't have to have the latest this, that and everything.

**How do you keep the relationship fresh?**

We're quite active, and there's always some project or thing we want to do together. We're at the age where it's not quite as sexually driven. As your hormones drop off your relationship changes and what you are thinking about becomes stimulating. I'm not talking in extremes. Of course we still have a great sexual life, but as your body changes so does your attitude. When you're younger, you're driven by lust. When you're older, other things begin to matter just as much.

**You have lived quite a unique lifestyle, and you now exude confidence and a grounded attitude. Where does your confidence as a woman come from?**

Spending my first two relationships trying to be someone that someone else wanted me to be, and then having all that time as a single mother where I suddenly had to do everything on my own without consulting someone else, empowered me. I got a teaching degree, bought a house, and raised my two girls all on my own. Everything was my responsibility. Over the years, those experiences helped me develop strength as a confident woman.

Maybe it's the maturity of my years, although I've never been shy. My father had quite an impact on me. Back in the 70s he said to me, "You can do anything you want." I remember him also saying, "Make sure you have sex before you get married, otherwise you won't know what you're getting yourself into." His openness definitely significantly influenced me. He was unusual for his time. Also, I lived around the world a lot – the Middle East, Caribbean, England, Scotland, Wales, Australia. Going to lots of different schools and being thrown into different situations, I developed an ability to perhaps be more confident than some of my peers. I remember in Grade 9 organising my own ballet school in the school yard.

I'm not sure how much of my confidence now is personality related, or background and upbringing. It's a combination of both I guess.

**What things do you consider are critical for a successful relationship?**

1. Aligned Personal Values.
2. Respect.
3. Affection / attachment.
4. Good sexual chemistry.
5. Enjoying doing things together. It doesn't have to be every single thing, but you must have a good basis of shared interests.
6. Sharing similar parenting styles.
7. Humour is huge – you must have a shared ability to laugh over things.
8. Communication obviously. Being able to mutually express differing opinions and views in a supportive environment.
9. Supporting each other; equal enthusiasm for each other's hopes and dreams.
10. Commitment to making things work together.

When I met Hugh all these things became apparent very quickly. When it's right, it's obvious. Hugh's daughter is gorgeous. Our blended kids all get on very well together. I'm very happy that my step-daughter is my step-daughter, and she's very happy that I am her step-mother.

**What advice would you give someone who is newly single, and fearful?**

Concentrate on being yourself, and do things that you want to do. If you try too hard at things, they usually don't work out. Being relaxed is important. Once you meet the right person, issues just slip away and it's easy. I believe that there is not one right person, but there are a lot of people who could be the right person if you let them be. Sometimes we expect too much. Realise that nothing is perfect.

**What are the warning signs that someone isn't right for you?**

1. That you have very different ideas on things that matter; eg. the way you treat people, politics, racial prejudice, money, things that are important to you but unimportant to them. If they are at the other end of the scale to you on important issues, then you have a problem. Depending on how important those things are to you, they could be a trigger or warning point.
2. If I was in a relationship where I found myself being undermined, or my opinions weren't important, or that feeling of an unequal balance, superiority / inferiority, or lots of arguments – those would all be warning signs for me.
3. Physical threat obviously – there are no excuses, it's not acceptable.
4. Not feeling comfortable in saying what you want to say.
5. Feeling like you are not being listened to; that your opinions don't matter.

**What did you teach your girls in regards to relationships?**

1. I tried very hard not to colour their relationship with their father.
2. I always included them in my relationships; I didn't particularly shield them from meeting suitors.
3. Tolerance.
4. People are different.
5. That being able to stand back and observe how a relationship is developing when you are getting to know someone is a good habit to develop.

**What is next for you and Hugh?**

There is still so much we want to do together, and we're trying to find the time to fit it all in. There are so many places to see and so many things to enjoy. Work gets in the way. We're looking forward to doing more travel, and remaining in good health. As you get older you start appreciating more what you've got. You make the most of it while you can. Next week we're going up to the mid north NSW coast and having a good get together with friends at Tuckers Rocks and Bongil Bongil National Park. We're also going to Lord Howe Island in July – Mum bought us that as my sixtieth birthday present.

# Author's Notes

90% of people I interviewed while researching for this book had learned from their experiences the veracity of what Relationships Educator Robyn Donnelly told us in Chapter 2, that while sexual chemistry is important, even more important are shared Personal Values, interests and life goals. They don't all have to be the same, but there has to be just as good a chemistry in these areas as there is sexually.

What does chemistry mean in this instance?

There has been some talk throughout the Shared Stories about Critical Personal Values and Negotiable Personal Values. Have you started considering what your own Critical and Negotiable Personal Values are? There are no right and wrong answers – simply whatever is right for you. Obvious Critical Values might involve do/don't want children, do/don't want marriage, the type of relationship you'd need your new partner to have with your children for you to be happy. Negotiable Personal Values might include hobbies. For instance, you might love doing up cars. You don't mind if your future partner doesn't want to put on a pair of overalls and join you, so long as they don't resent the time you're going to want to spend in the garage pursuing your interest. You have some room to negotiate if they are understanding of your passion. Important things to consider in understanding Critical Values include family relationships, relationships with friends, socialising, amount of together and alone time in love relationships, religion, finances, home life, career, hobbies and interests, health and fitness, commitment, politics, communication styles, leisure activities, lifestyle and anything else that's important to you. Be clear on the definition of Critical; ie. a deal breaker - it is so important to you that you have no room to negotiate on that issue. Obviously, you don't want everything in the Critical pile!

Self-Reflection Exercise 5 in Section 3 guides you through identifying your Critical and Negotiable Personal Values.

# Key Points From Robyn's Chapter

1. You must know who you are before you seek a new partner.
2. Being able to stand back and observe how a relationship is developing when you're getting to know someone is a good habit to develop.
3. There must be equal support and enthusiasm for each other's Personal Values.

# Chapter 21

## Helen's Story

**Royal Australian Air Force Service Woman, Teacher and now a Masseuse, 47-year-old Helen is twenty years into a delightful relationship with the second man she fell in love with.**

My husband, Rick, was the quintessential handsome, tall, charming, exciting Naval Officer. He was a good person and he lived an exciting life travelling the world. I was in the Royal Australian Air Force (RAAF) at the time so it seemed like a perfect match.

I had this glamorous idea that I was marrying a sailor and it was all going to be wonderful seeing the world together. I don't know why I thought that. It was a silly thing to think. The reality was that we were apart a lot. His career always came first. In the five years we were married, we were physically together in the same place for about 12 months in total.

Every time Rick would return home from service, we would have this honeymoon period for a few weeks. There would be the glitz, glamour and fun of catching up with each other, and going to the movies, dinners and socialising with friends. We would have a wonderful time, but then he would leave again. Towards the end of his stints at home, our time together would 'crash' and we would start having problems just before he went away. It became distressing that we were unsettled each time he left. While he was away, we would talk about having counselling together, but we never did.

I'm somewhat of a feminist and never saw myself as a stay-at-home mum. I'd always been clear that I didn't want children and all of a sudden Rick started saying that we should have a family. That came out of left field for me, particularly since he was away so often. It's difficult enough raising a child in a 2-parent family, let alone on your own.

Rick was constantly seeking to do courses to improve his rank with the Navy, and improve himself. That was his main focus. There was never any discussion of him changing his work situation so that he wouldn't be away so often. If you wanted promotion in the Navy, you had to do sea time, so that was that. I couldn't see how kids could fit into that.

I struggled at times with his mother's impact on our relationship. She was extremely negative about me. She would say degrading things about me being English and from the North, and about me being from a working class family, not middle class.

Rick's mother had left the family home when he was only 5-years-old and he hadn't seen or heard from her again until he was 15. He was quite damaged by this, and during our relationship I observed that he was worried about losing her again, so he seemed desperate to please her.

As a young girl in my early twenties, all of these issues were difficult for me. There were warning signs about some of these problems before we married; particularly the issues around his mother, but I ignored them. Before I married, I assumed that a marriage was simply between husband and wife, not that you're actually buying into a whole new family in addition to your husband. That was a mistake on my part, because, in fact, you do.

Rick was a good person. I'm a good person. However, we ended up damaging each other emotionally because we were wrong for each other.

When we separated I think it was mutual, but in the sense that I pushed for it. I knew that the relationship wasn't heading in the direction that it needed to be. Our divorce was fairly amicable. I didn't go after his superannuation, which I was advised that legally I could. I couldn't see how that would be fair. We simply divided the assets we had together. When you're in the armed services you don't accumulate too much because you move so regularly.

We cut off contact after our divorce, however, I've had contact with him as recent as months ago. He's no longer in the Navy but he is still with a maritime service. He loves what he does. It was good for us to exchange some emails after all that time had passed (21 years). We were able to lay some ghosts to rest and it was good for both of us. For instance, I expressed regret that I didn't have the maturity at the time to stand up for myself to his mother. He expressed regret that he didn't stand up to her on my behalf. He also told me that when I said I didn't want children, he thought I was joking. He married again, but he never did have children, and he would have liked to. I wish that had of happened for him, but perhaps things happen for a reason, because he's living his dream job, travelling between countries, and perhaps that wouldn't have been possible with kids. Who knows? Even though he didn't have kids, he is happy now.

I was 28-years-old when my marriage ended, and even though I had known for 12 – 18 months beforehand that things were going horribly wrong and my marriage was going to end, it was still very difficult when it did. I grieved deeply. When I got married, I thought I was going to live the rest of my life with that person. Now I was a divorcee. I never wanted to be a divorcee! I certainly felt the stigma in that, and also the loss of my fairytale love story.

Everything happened all at once. My marriage broke up, I left the RAAF, I went to full-time study to be a teacher, and I moved house because obviously I didn't want to remain in the marital home.

My financial situation had changed rather dramatically. I no longer had my RAAF salary. Now I was a full-time student working part-time jobs to support myself. I had $55,000 – my share of the marital assets – as a deposit to buy a house. Wanting to remain in the city, I looked at units instead of houses because they were more affordable. However, my home and garden are important to me. So I made a rather momentous decision at the time to move out of the city and into a suburb in a lower socio-economic area where I was able to get a house on a quarter of an acre within my price range. It turned out to be the best thing for me.

The thought of another relationship scared me. I never lost interest in men as such, but I wasn't interested in a relationship. I went to university, enjoyed my garden and friends, and worked my jobs. That was it really, that was my life. A simple life, and I enjoyed it. I enjoyed being single. I had jobs as a security guard, performing night fill at Woolworths, and then the final job I got while studying was with the local sports complex where I was the rink supervisor for the roller skating rink, pool and gym supervisor, and ran the kids holiday program. I also joined the local church near my new house, and found that good.

What happened next is still something of a mystery.

My long-time friend, Andy, visited, and quite inexplicably for us, romantic feelings developed.

Andy was a RAAF buddy of mine. We'd been good friends for over nine years. No sexual attraction at all. We genuinely were simply great buddies to each other. He supported me through my separation, moving and buying my own house, and moving on with my life. He was living in Queensland and I was in Perth at the time so he supported me over the phone.

After a time, he came to Perth to visit me. Partly as a holiday for himself, and partly to see what my new life was all about. Andy is a good friend to have. He genuinely cares for and takes an active interest in all his friends' lives.

When I saw him get off the plane there was an unexpected flutter inside me. I can't tell you why. There was nothing different about him to have caused it. When I felt the spark, I thought, "Oh, this is interesting and unexpected."

Andy was staying at my house; in a separate room of course. However, we had both felt the change towards each other. We were chatting one night, and that great song *Lady* came on my record player. I replayed it because it reminded me of Andy as he had always been my knight in shining armour. After that happened, we talked about the fact that we now had feelings for each other, but we were both concerned that if we took the next step to romance we might damage this wonderful, deep friendship that we had. We ended up parrying this topic of conversation around for a couple of months before we kissed.

During the difficult stages of my separation, my church minister, who was also a marriage counsellor, had loaned me a book. I can't remember the title, but the essence of the book was defining your bottom line in what you are not negotiable about in relationships, and what you are able to negotiate on. If there was one lesson I learnt from my marriage, it's certainly how important this is. It doesn't matter how lovely two people are, if they aren't suited, it ultimately won't work.

Reading that book, I had ascertained for myself what my 'not negotiables' were. I knew I needed someone who was accepting of my Christianity. I didn't need him to be a Christian, but he needed to be sympathetic and supportive to the fact that I was. He also needed to not want children obviously. I also wanted him to like cats. That might sound rather petty on the surface, but it has a deeper meaning for me. I believe there are control issues in people who don't like cats. I think they don't like them because they can't control them like they can control a dog, and that need for control carries on into other aspects of life. I also needed someone who had some kind of financial security, and wasn't someone who had simply drunk and drugged his way through life and had had a great time, but had not developed any sort of asset base.

My friend, Andy, passed all of my 'not negotiables', and I passed his.

It wasn't until just before Andy returned to Queensland that we decided to take it to the next level and see where it would go. We'd had a couple of months together and realised that things were quite comfortable. We weren't doing that honeymoon thing and then crashing like I had with my ex. The opposite was true with Andy and I. We had a nice, peaceful time together and a calm, steady relationship. That might sound boring to some people, but I love stability. It's amazing how we change as we mature. When we're young, we think the bad boys are all exciting, but in reality there's not enough substance to them. They don't cut it for a long-term relationship.

**What have you learned about relationships?**

1. That stability and security within a relationship are good things.
2. Substance requires mutual respect and a sharing of Personal Values. You don't have to have all the same Personal Values. If they have a sympathy and understanding towards something that's important to you, and they're prepared to support you in your Personal Values, then that can be okay too.
3. Laughter and simply enjoying each other's company are critically important. Andy and I absolutely crack each other up. A sense of humour is a great thing to have, and to keep and hold onto.

**What have you learned about being single after a major break-up?**

1. That it's okay to be single. That you actually discover things about yourself, and find strengths that you didn't know you had.

2. Don't be too hard on yourself. It's okay to grieve. Get some help if you need it; whether it's counselling or a trusted friend. But definitely don't sit at home and mull and ponder and get depressed and drink too much and cry too much. Don't feel alone, because you aren't alone.
3. If you're shy or unhappy, fake it until you make it. Get out there and be involved. Stick with it. I've joined some churches where nobody spoke to me at first, but eventually people get used to you and start talking. There are so many things out there to do, and groups to join to do them; eg. bushwalking, nature study, TAFE courses, book appreciation groups. There are also plenty of great organisations looking for volunteers. Volunteering is a great way to get yourself out there with a purpose.

**How does one make the most of being single?**

Don't sit at home. Explore as much as you can your own hobbies and interests. Join clubs and organisations. Work shouldn't be your defining factor, I believe. Try to do things outside of that. Bowling, dancing, some sort of short TAFE course … Meet new people. I would emphasise that it's about developing who you are. That kind of self-exploration can only happen by doing the things you like doing, with people who have similar interests to you. That's why clubs, groups and organisations can be a good thing. I have a single friend who is into dirt bike riding so he got a group around him and entered the Tatts Finke Desert Race. He didn't meet a girlfriend out in the Northern Territory, but he had the time of his life with like-minded people and certainly felt alive. Exploring your interests is so much more productive than clubbing and drinking. I think if you rely on pubs and clubs you'll likely not meet the kind of people who'll give you long-term satisfaction.

**Did you take any baggage from your first relationship into your second?**

Definitely. There was some sexual stuff, and some anger issues. After my marriage broke up, I was angry that I'd been put into the role of the perfect Stepford wife when that wasn't where I wanted to be. I was quite eager to not repeat that in my new relationship. I battled against it, and poor Andy copped it for a while until we worked through it.

**In regards to baggage, what did you do that you shouldn't have, and how did you work through it?**

I kept comparing Andy to my ex. It's not something you should do, but I think we all do it. I did it both in my head, and in some things I said out loud. Andy has this amazing ability to be wise and most of the time he's able to sit down quite calmly and analyse and talk about what just happened. He pulled me up on it, and we talked it through.

Then there was the sexual stuff. Dad used to wrestle with me when I was a girl, and he would get me to the point where I was hysterical and didn't want to play anymore. Then, he would proceed to lick me all around my neck and ears. He thought it was hilarious. It was never sexual or untoward or anything like that, but it was revolting, and a control thing.

Unfortunately, my ex, Rick, did a similar thing; also thinking it was hilarious.

By the time I entered into a relationship with Andy, I couldn't stand to have my neck or ears kissed. That took a few years to work through. We talked and talked and talked as things would crop up, and then we trialled a few things, and eventually I was able to work through my emotions and not find kissing in that area gross anymore. It's a stupid thing, but it is what it is, and it was important to me.

**Did Andy bring any baggage into your relationship?**

Yes. Andy had serious health issues with his back. He was no longer able to work, and this was likely to be a permanent situation. He was worried that he would be a burden to me with his back injuries and mobility issues. I chose to be with Andy because he's such a joy to be around. He had some trouble accepting that.

There was one other thing. Leaving the RAAF had been traumatic for Andy. He was forced out after being permanently affected from an operation. It was absolutely devastating for him. One of his ways of coping was to collect militaria objects and acquire books. It got a little out of hand, and somewhat overtook our home. We talked through all that and eventually found a reasonable solution that suited us both.

It's so very important to talk things through. Once you start a conversation, you usually discover deeper reasons than are evident on the surface.

**How do you keep a relationship healthy 20 years in?**

1. You always have to be honest. You need to always feel safe to talk to the other person about what you're feeling. Having said that though, you do need to separate your emotions from the issue and speak calmly and carefully. It's easy to lash out and be cruel to people. I think many people say things without thought.
2. People need to pause. That helps to keep a relationship good. Pausing and thinking, "Am I doing this just because I've had a crap day and feel bad, or is this something that genuinely needs to be said?"
3. There has got to be mutual respect within the relationship. With my ex, I had little respect for him towards the end because he was doing exactly what he wanted to do all the time, and expected me to simply come on board.
4. Relationships have to be give and take; a mutual respect to ensure that you give to each other all the time. Both people's needs are important and need to be met.
5. When you're in a relationship, wider families can play a huge part. The movie *Meet The Parents* portrays it well when they talk about the inner circle, the outer circle, and the Circle of Trust. It's important that you and your partner are the inner Circle of Trust and decision

making. It has got to be only the two of you in that innermost circle. Even if you have children, they must be the next layer out from you and your partner. Extended family need to be the next layer again. Andy and I had to work hard on this, on both sides. I had to make a conscious shift in my thinking. There are wider family who need to be acknowledged and respected, but they do need to be kept firmly in their place and not intrude on the relationship. It's up to Andy to keep his family in their place, and up to me to keep my family in their place.

6. Relationships are about give and take. Just be on the lookout that it's not you doing all the giving, and them doing all the taking.

## Author's Notes

Helen gives great examples of defining your bottom line (ie. Personal Values) in what you're not negotiable about in relationships and what you are able to negotiate on. This should have given you some food for thought for your own Critical and Negotiable Personal Values.

# Key Points From Helen's Chapter

1. Being single is about developing who you are. You discover things about yourself, and find strengths you didn't know you had.
2. Don't feel alone, because you aren't alone. It's okay to be single.
3. When meeting new people be on the lookout that it's not you doing all the giving, and them doing all the taking.

# Now, On To You ...

## Self-Reflection Exercises

Many times throughout the Shared Stories, speakers suggested that you mend your broken heart, love yourself, know who you are, and be doing the things that you're interested in, before you fall in love again. However, as mentioned in Bernie's story, it's much easier to talk in hindsight. These can all be challenging to achieve.

Go easy on yourself. Don't expect to change all that you might want to change overnight. Allow yourself time to grieve all that your grief encompasses. There is not one specific road map for success. Your life is your journey, and yours alone. Ultimately, you are the best person to know what is right for you, and to know when you are ready to move forward onto a new step. My wish for you is simply that the Shared Stories and guidance in this book help you to move forward with confidence, and perhaps give you ideas on how to get moving past a point at which you might be stuck.

Employ 'chunking down' techniques. Goal setting is a powerful tool that you can use to move your life from where you are at this very moment, to where you want to be in the near future. And chunking your goals down into small, achievable steps to get there is a valuable tool to remember.

However, there are a few misnomers circulating about how easy it is to achieve goals. For instance, some people say that if you simply 'believe' something strong enough, that it will come to pass. I'm sorry to have to be the one to break it to you, but if you simply lay in bed all day 'believing' that the perfect partner and the ideal life is about to find you and sweep you off your feet, then you are likely to be quite disappointed.

Michelle Bridges and Jamie Oliver have not built their extraordinarily successful empires because they 'believed' luck was going to come their way. They are successful because they have a vision, and they work hard to make their vision a reality. To achieve great things, of course positive thinking is necessary, but you have to couple it with *Action*. Bridges and Oliver aren't lucky, they're hard working and committed. How much do you desire an ideal love relationship? Are you willing to put in the effort to make it happen?

There is another important point to acknowledge about successful people. Not everything goes their way! Things go wrong, but they don't let setbacks keep them down. They evaluate the experience and learn from it, and use that experience to move onto bigger and better things. Life is one big learning experience, and it's how you pick yourself up and move on that will define you.

Need more proof? In 2000 and to a long standing ovation, Michael J Fox left his beloved TV sitcom, *Spin City*, because his Parkinson's Disease had become too much to continue full-time acting. He could have given up. Instead, since 2000, Fox has written three books:

1. *Lucky Man: A Memoir* (2002)
2. *Always Looking Up: The Adventures of an Incurable Optimist* (2009)
3. *A Funny Thing Happened on the Way to the Future: Twists and Turns and Lessons Learned* (2010).

In 2010, he was awarded a Doctorate in Medicine degree for his work towards finding a cure for Parkinson's Disease.

What you do next will define you – both to yourself and others. You are a unique individual, and now is your chance to re-group, reflect, and explore your ideal life without the clutter of meeting other's needs. As Carlos said in Chapter 5 … "take a new picture". What a simply divine opportunity.

The exercises offered here will help you reflect on your past achievements and your past challenges, and in so doing help you to identify your goals moving forward. Do the exercises in this book, and by the time you get to the end, you will have a strong vision of the life you wish to lead, including the qualities you are looking for in your next relationship. You will have also explored what you have to offer to a new partner, and what type of person will best appreciate and grow with you.

These exercises were developed for Goal Setting Workshops which I run at Creative Health Retreats.

Take your time – it is suggested you do no more than one exercise a week – to allow time for reflection on the insights you uncover as you work through the exercises.

# EXERCISE 1 – Year in Review

It's important to keep things in perspective. It's easy to focus on any negatives, but not everything in your life is a disaster. Write down all the happy/good things that have happened in your life over the past year; everything that you're grateful for. For example, someone may have surprised you with something nice, a mate came over and made you laugh on a difficult day, achievements at work, people close to you with whom you have fulfilling relationships, etc. Take your time; capture everything – it's a celebration.

Secondly, write down all the challenges you've had in the past year. Royal stuff-ups through to things that were simply disappointing because they didn't live up to your expectations. There may even be an area in your life that continually fails to live up to your expectations; eg. dating, your relationship with your boss, relationship with your family, can't lose weight, etc.

Thirdly, make lists of these things:

- Your five greatest strengths
- Your five greatest weaknesses
- Repeated mistakes
- Skills you need to improve.

Tuck your answers away. We'll come back to them again later.

**EXAMPLE – Assumed character Michelle**

---

**Good things that happened**

1. Nominated employee of the month at work.
2. Surprised at how much my brother was there for me after my marriage broke up.
3. Been talking more to some colleagues who've been through a marriage break-up and they've now become friends.
4. Re-discovered my love of music – have been playing guitar a lot more.
5. Went to a Legends of Rock concert at a vineyard with people from work and it was an awesome night.
6. Started keeping a journal and am finding it therapeutic.
7. Read *Finding Love Again* and it gave me some great insights into myself and the next relationship I want ☺
8. Found out that I can get 5 free counselling sessions through my work's Employee Assistance Program.
9. Got a big tax return.
10. Am loving my new apartment in the city.
11. My sister randomly sent me flowers one day to let me know she's there for me.
12. When Dad cried because I was crying when I told him my ex, Max, left me, I realised just how much my Dad loves me.
13. I've found I absolutely love going to the movies on my own – there's no-one crunching popcorn in my ear.

(Write as many as you can think of)

**Things that didn't go so well**

1. My marriage broke up.
2. The settlement is still dragging on and is stressful. Max is being deliberately difficult.
3. Got too drunk at some work functions because I felt weird being there as a single. Wasn't a great look.
4. My ex's family don't want anything to do with me. I don't understand it. They were my family too for 6 years.
5. My best friend sucks – won't come out with me, too busy with her own husband and kids.
6. I've seen that divorced guys get looked after by friends and their friends' wives, but divorced women get seen as a threat by some other women and are excluded from invitations. What's that all about?!
7. Keep trying to lose weight but haven't lost any yet.

**My 5 greatest strengths**

1. Guitar and music in general.
2. I'm great at remembering names.
3. I'm a good listener and make people feel good about themselves.
4. Loyalty.
5. I'm funny.

**My 5 greatest weaknesses**

1. Public speaking.
2. Shy when in a group of new people.
3. Get repeatedly hurt by people not being loyal.
4. Too soft on myself where food and exercise are concerned.
5. Keep lending money to people who don't pay me back.

**Repeated mistakes**

1. Getting hurt by others. Maybe it's because I spend more time pleasing others than pleasing myself.
2. Diet fails.
3. Not speaking up about my needs in a relationship.
4. Lending money.
5. 3 times in the last year I've reversed my car into something – what's that all about?

**Skills I need to improve**

1. Stress management.
2. Public speaking.
3. Taking care of my physical health – my attitude towards food and exercise needs to change. I reach for food for comfort at the moment. How do I make myself truly believe 'my body is my temple'?
4. Standing up for myself. Knowing myself. I spend so much time pleasing others I'm not sure I truly, truly know what my Critical and Negotiable Personal Values are.
5. Money management.

# EXERCISE 2 – Modelling

This one is a simple question, but your answers should be considered and full.

Who are the people around you who are in good relationships? For each couple, write down all that you have observed that makes their relationship good. You might even ask them what they believe are the keys to their successful relationship.

I encourage you to share the answers via the *Finding Love Again* Facebook page.

**Example – Michelle**

There are only 2 relationships I know of that I think are really working well.

---

**Mum & Dad**

1. They make each other laugh.
2. They give each other compliments.
3. They still genuinely 'like' each other. They love spending time with us kids, but they also like spending time just the two of them.
4. They don't put each other down.
5. Mum makes a fuss over making Dad his favourite meals, and Dad still brings Mum bunches of flowers.
6. They still hold hands.
7. They've told me that when they disagree about us kids they discuss it in private, not in front of us.
8. They're very open with each other; they talk about everything.
9. Mum makes us do this thing where over dinner when we get

together as a family we have to tell each other the best thing that happened to us that week, and the worst thing. Mum tells me that her and Dad do that every night when they're alone.

10. They're not mean to each other, even when they're angry. They talk to each other respectfully.
11. They 'play' together. They like seeing stand-up comedians together, and they still play practical jokes on each other.

---

**Karli & Ben**

1. They're both mad keen football fans and much of their lives revolve around playing touch footy, supporting the local NRL club and travelling to big games.
2. They talk respectfully to each other. I've not seen them put each other down.
3. They're physically affectionate. Not in a gross way – it's sweet.
4. I know they've talked about their individual goals and their joint goals for their lives together.
5. They work well as a team. They share the housework, they've invested in property together, they share the cooking, they entertain as a well-oiled team.
6. Karli has told me they've been to counselling together a couple of times when they've been through a rough patch.
7. They support each other in their careers. Karli regularly entertains Ben's staff, and Ben has used his contacts to get Karli subjects to interview when she's needed them for news articles.
8. Because Ben's Catholic, they had to go to pre-marriage education before they got married. Karli said they explored each other's Personal Values and talked about things they

hadn't talked about before – like whether they should have separate or joint bank accounts after they got married, where the kids should go school, and heaps of other things. Karli said it was good – they found they thought quite differently about some things at first but worked through to compromises.

9. They genuinely care about each other – it's obvious in the way they look out for each other, and are considerate to each other.
10. They have fun together.
11. They spend a lot of their time together, but they also go out alone with their own friends occasionally too.
12. They like each other's families.

# EXERCISE 3 – Letting Go

People can bring us our greatest pain, but they can also bring us our greatest happiness.

You deserve to own all your power, and not to give it away, at your expense, to people from your past. Sometimes we can beat ourselves up too long. Just because you were the wrong person for someone, doesn't mean that you're the wrong person for everyone. There are others out there with similar Personal Values and desires as yourself, and those people will connect with you. Be strong. Own your past experiences, and move into your future.

Embrace happiness. Open yourself to the unrestrained joy that you deserve to experience through healthy relationships with awesome people in your life. They are out there. Some will already be in your life, and some new ones are coming your way.

You know when you have good people around you, because around them you are the best version of yourself. There is a saying I like, "Before you diagnose yourself with depression or low self-esteem firstly check that you are not, in fact, surrounded by assholes," (William Gibson). A strong support network goes a long way towards aiding our emotional stability. If you don't have a strong support network within your inner circle, consider moving your focus towards people who are more supportive and positive towards you.

This exercise is for those of you who like to write. For those of you who aren't big writers, try dot points.

This story is about yourself and your relationships. It need only be 500 words but you can write more if you desire. The title is *Letting Go.*

Start by describing the key relationships that have defined who you are. It doesn't have to be a literary masterpiece so don't get hung up on writing quality. This story is for your eyes only, unless you choose to share it with anyone.

Next in your story I want you to write, *Today I made a decision to let go of negative emotions holding me back. I don't regret one moment of my past because it has made me the thoughtful, calm, strong person I am today. I've had great experiences and bad ones, and I own them all because now I look to the future with excitement. I have learned about relationships that ... (fill in the blanks). In my future I see ... (describe your ideal relationship and what you will be doing together).*

Happy writing. Have fun with it. Cleanse, and begin looking towards the future with a smile on your face.

Having trouble getting started? Try these words, 'Today, I look back over my past relationships, and this is what leaps out at me …'

Or

'I am ?? years-old and this is what I have learnt about relationships …'

**Michelle's Example**

**Letting Go**

My Mum and Dad have an awesome relationship. I grew up in a great family where there was respect and genuine caring for each other and yet I went and married someone who wasn't right for me. Our relationship was all about Max, and what he needed to be happy. Looking back, I felt sorry for him because his brother died in a car accident when they were teenagers, his mother died of cancer when he was in his twenties, and his Dad was a shell of a man who didn't take much interest in Max's life. Max is good looking, strong, enigmatic and sardonic. He's all-round sexy. I wanted to show him everything a family could be, and the pure happiness that a good relationship brings to one's life. But that's not what Max wanted. Max put me down a lot. To be fair to him, he probably didn't appreciate my trying to change him. He found my closeness with my family weird and claustrophobic. He didn't want to talk about things in his life or mine. He liked to keep things inside and simply go about being popular. He kept most people at a distance, preferring acquaintances to spending a lot of time with the same people. Max resented me trying to change his ways. He liked his life just the way it was. His insults and jabs have affected my self-confidence. I thought when two people fell in love that everything else just fell into place. How wrong was I? We had very different Personal Values and very different desires for the future of our relationship. I'm angry at him for not being the person I thought he could be, but mostly I'm angry at myself for thinking I could make him someone he wasn't. He put me down even when we were first dating but I always told myself he was a hurt man and I was going to cure that hurt.

However, today I'm making a decision to let go of negative emotions holding me back. I don't regret one moment of my past because it has made me the thoughtful, calm, strong person I am today. I've had great experiences and bad ones, and I own them all because now I look to the future with excitement. I have learned about relationships that:

1. You shouldn't view people through rose-coloured glasses, or assume they hold the same Personal Values. Instead, I need to ask open-ended questions and listen, as well as step back and observe behaviours, to find out what their Personal Values are so I can make a considered decision as to whether we're compatible.
2. I shouldn't ignore early warning signs that someone isn't right for me.
3. Just because I think someone needs to be fixed, doesn't mean they want to be fixed, or even that they need fixing at all. Not everyone has the same Personal Values as me.
4. There is a healthy and an unhealthy way to communicate and argue in relationships. When you're with the right person you are free to express yourself without negative judgement.
5. Making the decision to enter into a long-term relationship is a fleeting moment amongst the years that follow. It's therefore a very important decision, and I deserve happiness.

In my future I see a relationship where:

1. I'm smiling far more than I'm sad.
2. We enjoy music together.

3. We communicate openly, honestly and respectfully.
4. We have a solid friendship base.
5. We goal-set together.
6. We make each laugh.
7. We're affectionate.
8. We spend time together, but also apart with our own friends – a happy balance we both enjoy.
9. We're married and raise our kids in a nurturing, positive environment where values of family, social conscience and caring for others are priorities.

# EXERCISE 4 – Taking Action

The difference between goal setting that works, and goal setting that doesn't, is discipline.

Being a writer, my favourite quote is by the author Stephen King: "I only write when I'm inspired, and I make sure I'm inspired at 9am every week day." Consistently reading that quote got me off my butt to complete my first book, *Inspiring IVF Stories*. 'Chunking down' the workload helped me complete the mammoth task of writing a book.

Life isn't a breeze for *anyone*. Sure, different people have different challenges, but *everyone* has them. What defines you, is the way that you respond to the challenges that life presents you. Are you a winner, a quitter or a coaster?

In Exercise 1 you were asked to write down your greatest strengths, greatest weaknesses and repeated mistakes. There was a reason for this.

Winners are not winners because they never lose. Winners are winners because they work hard, commit to a passion, and they learn from their mistakes. Do you think it's always the tennis player with the hardest forehand who wins? No, of course not. Sometimes it's the player with the average forehand, but the smarts to alter their game to engineer circumstances where they get to maximise the use of their killer backspin. The key to winning is maximising your assets and minimising your weaknesses. It can be easy to focus on what we *aren't* good at, and in so doing, miss opportunities for maximising what we *are* good at.

Go back now to your answers from Exercise 1, and consider the repeated mistakes, greatest strengths and greatest weaknesses that you wrote down. Give some thought as to how these have affected your past relationships and/or dating attempts. Write down how they have enhanced your relationships and attempts at love, and how they have hindered you.

In terms of *Finding Love*, spend some time considering how you might be under-utilising your greatest strengths and come up with ways for you to maximise those strengths. For instance, in a group situation you might be engaging and people are drawn to you, whereas you might be average at presenting yourself in written form. In this case, in a dating sense, internet dating might not work for you. 'Dinner for 6' or something similar might be more suitable for you. Perhaps you're great at sport, but not the funniest person in the singles pool, so inviting people you're interested in on sports-related dates might help you to relax and be yourself.

Things don't change, only you can change. "If you continue doing the same things, don't be surprised when you continue getting the same results," (anonymous). Consider your repeated mistakes. Is there something in your life you need to change? Is it something you can change on your own or do you need to seek additional help?

To give yourself the best chance of *Finding Love*:

1. Maximise your strengths.
2. Minimise your weaknesses.
3. Learn from your repeated mistakes.
4. Check and change patterns of behaviour that are not serving you well.

**Example – Michelle**

**Qualities**

| **Strengths:** | **Weaknesses:** | **Repeated Mistakes:** |
|---|---|---|
| Guitar and music in general. | Public speaking. | Getting hurt by others. |
| I'm great at remembering names. | Shy when in a group of new people. | Diet fails. |
| I'm a good listener and make people feel good about themselves. | Get repeatedly hurt by people not being loyal. | Not speaking up about my needs in a relationship. |
| Loyalty. | Too soft on myself where food and exercise are concerned. | Lending money. |
| I'm funny. | Keep lending money to people who don't pay me back. | 3 times in the last year I've reversed my car into something. |

**How these have hindered my love relationships**

| | | |
|---|---|---|
| Tend to listen and give more than I take – this can mean I'm not being true to myself or my partner by not speaking up about my own needs. | I'm not feeling sexy because I'm carrying a few extra kilos and not particularly fit. | Haven't communicated my needs well in relationships which has ultimately led to dissatisfaction on their part and mine. |
| | It frustrates people around me when I let others take advantage of me. | Relying too much on emotion rather than fact has seen me make some bad decisions. |
| | I'm often worried about what others think. | |

**How these have benefitted my love relationships**

People enjoy being around me.

I can be a lot of fun.

Loyalty, and therefore commitment, is a good trait to have in relationships – I don't walk away easily.

---

**How to maximise the opportunity**

Explore local music groups / bands to meet like-minded people.

Monitor relationships to ensure the giving/taking is equally balanced – concentrate on those friendships and relationships where the balance goes both ways.

Reflect on what my Critical and Negotiable Personal Values are in a relationship so that I can express them.

Implement a healthy and gradual eating and exercise plan. Join diet and exercise groups to keep motivated and meet people with similar interest. Chunk my goals down so they're achievable. Losing weight and getting fitter will make me feel good.

Join Toastmasters – I'll meet new people and conquering a fear will boost my self-esteem.

Research alternative therapies and/or meditation to work towards understanding why I'm always trying to 'fix' people instead of enjoying them the way they are.

Manage stress better – try yoga/meditation, and if this doesn't work perhaps bushwalking – with bushwalking I'd be killing 2 birds with one stone – relaxing and losing weight.

Practise stepping back and taking an unemotional view of relationships now and again to evaluate how they're going.

# EXERCISE 5 – Personal Values

You're now going to write that magical list of what you're looking for in a partner. To do so, you first need to identify your own Critical (Non-Negotiable) and Negotiable Personal Values.

There are no right and wrong answers. Individuals' Personal Values differ. Keep in mind, however, that there are 'nice to have' things in a relationship – like drives a hot car, likes red wine, is a dog person, etc. – that whilst nice, do not make a relationship endure. A lack of knowing and/or acknowledging of your Critical Personal Values, and therefore not connecting them to your choices and actions, leads you to engage in relationship insanity – repeatedly doing the same thing / going out with the same type of person, and expecting a different answer. Critical Personal Values are about what you *need*, as opposed to what you like to have.

You know when you're living your life in harmony with your Critical Personal Values because life feels … right. If things are feeling … off, and you're not quite sure why, this is a great exercise for you.

It is a good idea to evaluate your Personal Values every few years or whenever you feel 'unbalanced'. Whilst Personal Values are fairly stable, they may change depending on your life circumstances. For instance, when you first start your career you might find that money, challenge and promotion are high priorities for you, but after you have a family you might find that these Personal Values are superseded in importance by work/life balance.

The following is a comprehensive list of Personal Values to stimulate your thinking. Consider and tailor this list carefully from two perspectives. Firstly, Critical Personal Values for you in terms of what you need in a relationship. Secondly, Critical Personal Values in terms of what you need as an individual. Circle your Top 10 from each perspective. If something that is a deal breaker to you is not included in the table, add it in; eg. non-smoker, animal lover, non-drug user.

I've suggested you consider your Top 10 Critical Values from both a relationship perspective and an individual perspective to allow a holistic view. It's probable that something critical to you from a personal viewpoint, is not critical from a relationship viewpoint. For example, strenuous exercise / a high level of fitness might be critical to you personally, but from a relationship perspective you have room to negotiate because you don't mind if your partner is not an exercise fanatic like yourself, so long as they are accepting of your need for time to fit in your exercise schedule. Another such example might be that you're very close to your extended family and this is a Critical Personal Value to you, but you don't mind if your partner isn't as close to their own extended family, as long as they are understanding and supportive of your relationship with yours.

There are over 200 values in the list below. To help you narrow the list down, for both exercises; ie. Critical Relationship and Critical Personal - approach the list this way:

1. With a blue highlighter, mark the values that you immediately know are not important to you. This should eliminate around half of the values on the list.
2. With a yellow highlighter, mark those remaining qualities that are nice to have but not critical to you.
3. With an orange highlighter, mark all those remaining that you see as Critical to you. You might find that you still have a list of far more than 10 values, perhaps even up to 50.
4. Write each of the orange marked Values on a sticky note. You're now going to sort all of these sticky notes into 10 stacks by putting like values together. When you've narrowed it down to 10 stacks write a one-line value that captures the essence of the sticky notes in that stack. Still stuck? Reading Michelle's completed example below will assist.

5. Your Negotiable Personal Values will be evident with a similar exercise performed on your yellow highlighted values.

Accountability
Adaptability
Affection (Love & Caring)
Arts
Awareness
Belonging
Caring
Change & Variety
Close Relationships
Community
Competence
Consistency
Continuous Learning
Cooperation
Courage
Curiosity
Dependability
Dialogue
Discretion
Ease with Uncertainty
Economy
Elegance
Ethics
Environmental
Excitement
Expressiveness
Fame
Family – embraces extended family
Family – doesn't want children
Fidelity
Fitness
Forgiveness
Friendship – with friends/socialising
Generosity
Growth

Accuracy
Advancement & Promotion
Altruism
Assertiveness
Balance
Boldness
Carefulness
Cheerfulness
Coaching/Mentoring
Community Involvement
Competitiveness
Contentment
Contribution
Correctness
Courtesy
Decisiveness
Determination
Diligence
Diversity
Ecological Awareness
Effectiveness
Empathy
Enthusiasm
Equality
Expertise
Fairness
Family-oriented
Family – able to embrace children from previous marriage
Family – doesn't want marriage
Financial Stability
Fluency
Freedom
Fun
Goodness

Achievement
Adventure
Ambition
Attitude
Being the Best
Calmness
Challenge
Clear Mindedness
Commitment
Compassion
Conflict Resolution
Continuous Improvement
Control
Country
Creativity
Democracy
Devoutness
Discipline
Dynamism
Economic Security
Efficiency
Enjoyment
Entrepreneurial
Excellence
Exploration
Faith
Family – wants children and/or marriage
Family – doesn't have children from previous marriage
Fast-living
Financial Wealth
Focus
Friendship – with partner
Future Generations
Grace
Hard Work
Helping Society

| | | |
|---|---|---|
| Health | Happiness | Honour |
| Holiness | Helping Other People | Independence |
| Humour | Honesty | Inner Harmony |
| Influencing Others | Humility | Integrity |
| Inquisitiveness | Ingenuity | Intuition |
| Intelligence | Insightfulness | Job Security |
| Initiative | Intellectual Status | Justice |
| Job Tranquillity | Involvement | Legacy |
| Knowledge | Joy | Love |
| Listening | Leadership | Market Position |
| Loyalty | Location | Merit |
| Mastery | Making a Difference | Obedience |
| Money | Meaningful Work | Order |
| Open Communication | Nature | Patriotism |
| Originality | Openness | Perfection |
| Personal Fulfilment | Patience | Physical Challenge |
| Personal Development | Perseverance | Power & Authority |
| Pleasure | Piety | Privacy |
| Practicality | Positivity | Prudence |
| Professional Growth | Preparedness | Quality-oriented |
| Public Service | Professionalism | Responsibility |
| Religious | Purity | Recognition |
| Resourcefulness | Reliability | Risk-Taking |
| Restraint | Reputation | Self-Actualisation |
| Respect | Results-Oriented | Self-Respect |
| Safety | Rigour | Sensitivity |
| Self-Control | Security | Shrewdness |
| Selflessness | Self-Discipline | Sophistication |
| Serenity | Self-Reliance | Stability |
| Simplicity | Service | Strength |
| Speed | Soundness | Supervising Others |
| Status | Spontaneity | Temperance |
| Structure | Strategic | Thoughtfulness |
| Support | Success | Tolerance |
| Thankfulness | Teamwork | Trustworthiness |
| Time Freedom | Thoroughness | Uniqueness |
| Traditionalism | Timeliness | Vision |
| Trust-Seeking | Trust | Wellbeing |
| Unity | Understanding | Work with Others |

Vitality
Wisdom
Work Alone

Usefulness
Wealth
Work Under Pressure

Now place these in order until you have them prioritised from 1 through to 10 in each category. Limiting yourself to 10 Critical Personal Values aids in clarity.

You can now go on to write your full list of what you need and what you would like in your next relationship.

**Michelle's List**

---

**Critical – Relationship**

1. Family – children/marriage.
2. Friendship with partner.
3. Affection (love, caring, thoughtfulness, and sexual attraction).
4. Teamwork (equals in everything).
5. Respect.
6. Happiness, fun and laughter.
7. Adventure.
8. Open communication is practised and encouraged both ways (good listener as well as expressing their own needs).
9. Dependability / reliability /and financial security (ie. is in a similar position as myself).
10. Takes care of their health – Non-smoker, social drinker, exercises, balanced eating choices, not a regular drug user.

**Critical – Individual**

My new partner must be supportive and encouraging of my individual Critical Personal Values.

1. Being a good Mum and Wife.
2. Close to extended family.
3. A handful of quality, meaningful, close and loyal friends.
4. Humour / fun / adventure.
5. Fit and healthy.
6. Balance.
7. Calmness and clear mindedness.
8. Professional achievement and growth.
9. Making a difference / social conscience.
10. Belonging.

**Negotiable – relationship nice to haves**

1. Taller than me.
2. Gets on exceptionally well with my friends and family – ie. genuinely enjoys their company and wants to maximise time with them.
3. Has family and friends who I genuinely enjoy and want to hang out with.
4. Likes animals, especially cats, in particular, my cat.
5. Likes going to the beach, music, seeing bands play, playing tennis, going to the movies, seeing stand-up comedians, bushwalking, zoos, theme parks and exploring new things.
6. Can cook.
7. Enjoys a night in alone together drinking wine and playing board games just as much as partying with friends.
8. Makes me laugh really hard every day.
9. Is entrepreneurial, adventurous, positive and enthusiastic.
10. Has a great smile, cute bum, and mischievous eyes – smiles at me and listens to me like I'm the only girl in the world for

him.

11. Wears nice clothes.
12. Is a good driver.
13. Regularly compliments me.
14. Does half the house duties without me having to ask.
15. Is happy to financially support our family while we have children so I can be a full-time carer.
16. Likes trail bike riding and camping – and I feel safe being on the back of his bike.
17. Knows how to use a chainsaw and wants to live on acreage.
18. Is fun when they're drunk, and if they're not, that they acknowledge this and limit their alcohol intake.

# EXERCISE 6 – Your Story

To be an interesting person you have to have things to talk about and you have to be interested in what the other person says.

At a party, gathering, first date or when joining a new group, you are going to get asked, "So, what is your story?" A timeline of the most interesting things you have done in your life will help you articulate this in a fascinating way.

**Step 1:** Complete the Table below. You don't need to write something in every square, it's just piecing together a timeline of events. Start with your year of birth.

**Step 2:** Use a highlighter to mark the squares which you think will be most interesting to another person. This way when you articulate your story, you won't focus on the negative or boring stuff.

**Step 3:** Practise articulating the highlights into an interesting narrative of your life. Anecdotal snippets will serve you better in conversations than one long monologue. Most poignant, this exercise demonstrates how *un*interesting your previous break-up is in the totality of your life story.

## Michelle's Example

| YEAR | WHERE LIVING | WHAT DOING | AN ACHIEVEMENT | A PEOPLE THING | A FUNNY THING | LITTLE KNOWN FACT |
|---|---|---|---|---|---|---|
| 1971 | Newcastle | | Being born | | | |
| 1972 | | | | | | |
| 1973 | | | | | | |
| 1974 | | | | | | |
| 1975 | | | | | | |
| 1976 | | | | | | |
| 1977 | | | | | | |
| 1978 | | | | | | |
| 1979 | | | | Met my best friend in music class | | |
| 1980 | | | | | I won the school cross-country because the leading pack went the wrong way | |
| 1981 | | | | | | |
| 1982 | | Finished primary school | | | | |
| 1983 | | | | | | |
| 1984 | | | | | | Won first prize in a national poetry comp |
| 1985 | | | | | | |

| | | | | | | |
|---|---|---|---|---|---|---|
| 1986 | | | | My friends started a band called The Rock Girls – played all through high school | | |
| 1987 | | | Our band came third at High Schools Eisteddfod | | | Got a short story published in *That's Life* |
| 1988 | | Finished high school | Won the Eisteddfod | | | |
| 1989 | England | Degree in Political Science / Travel | | | My sister was on the toilet when the Newcastle Earthquake hit | Spoke to Princess Di at Harrods. She liked my accent. |
| 1990 | England | | Saw most of Europe | Still best friends with group from Uni – they've since visited Australia | | Jockeyed on Uni radio station |
| 1991 | England | | | | | |
| 1992 | Canberra | Worked for the Minister for Defence | | | | |
| 1993 | | | | | | |
| 1994 | | | | | | |
| 1995 | | | | | | |
| 1996 | | | | | | |
| 1997 | | | | | | |
| 1998 | | | Did the Mount Kilimanjaro trek and an African Safari | | | |

| 1999 | | | | | | |
|---|---|---|---|---|---|---|
| 2000 | Newcastle | Got a job as advisor for the State Member for Newcastle | | Met Max at a club | | |
| 2001 | | | | | | |
| 2002 | | | | | | |
| 2003 | | | | | | |
| 2004 | | My boss let me form a team from Newcastle to go over and help with clean up for Thailand tsunami | Spent 8 weeks in Thailand helping with clean up – mostly clearing debris and distributing water | Both the devastation and resilience of the people changed me as a person | | Max and I due to fly to Thailand the day after the Tsunami hit – had a profound effect on me |
| 2005 | | | Helped start 4 Newcastle – keeping the streets safe after dark | | | |
| 2006 | | | | | | |
| 2007 | | | | | | |
| 2008 | | | | | | |
| 2009 | | | Travelled to South Island of NZ | | Video of me paragliding off a mountain – had turrets. | |
| 2010 | | | | | | |
| 2011 | | | | | | |

| 2012 | | | | | Dad won $965 on Deal or No Deal and took us all to lunch at Noahs | |
|---|---|---|---|---|---|---|
| 2013 | | | We got the lock out laws passed in Newcastle | | | |
| 2014 | | Low self-esteem – first time in my life – really struggled with Max leaving me | | Max left me | | |
| 2015 | | | Got back into my music and wrote my first song in years | Started a singles Facebook group – it's been a Godsend – vineyard tours, tennis foursome | | |

After doing this exercise, I guess I'm more of a social activist that I'd realised.

# EXERCISE 7 – Your Action Plan

**Setting your relationship goal and chunking it down into achievable targets**

You've done all the work. Now fill out the table below with your own answers and you have your Personal Action Plan to Finding Love; a love that will endure and make you happy.

**Example Action Plan**

| | MICHELLE'S ACTION PLAN |
|---|---|
| **MY GOAL** | To be in a mutually supportive, encouraging and happy marriage. |
| **CRITICAL & NEGOTIABLE PERSONAL VALUES – the things I'm looking for** | **Critical – Relationship**<br>1. Family – children/marriage.<br>2. Friendship with partner.<br>3. Affection (love, caring, thoughtfulness, and sexual attraction).<br>4. Teamwork (equals in everything).<br>5. Respect.<br>6. Happiness, fun and laughter.<br>7. Adventure.<br>8. Open communication is practised and encouraged both ways (good listener as well as expressing their own needs).<br>9. Dependability / reliability /and financial security (ie. is in a similar position as myself). |

10. Takes care of their health – Non-smoker, social drinker, exercises, balanced eating choices, not a drug user.

---

**Critical – Individual**

My new partner must be supportive and encouraging of my individual Critical Personal Values.

1. Being a good Mum and Wife.
2. Close to extended family.
3. A handful of quality, meaningful, close and loyal friends.
4. Humour / fun / adventure.
5. Fit and healthy.
6. Balance.
7. Calmness and clear mindedness.
8. Professional achievement and growth.
9. Making a difference / social conscience.
10. Belonging.

---

**Negotiable – Nice to Haves**

1. Taller than me.
2. Gets on exceptionally well with my friends and family – ie. genuinely enjoys their company and wants to maximise time with them.
3. Has family and friends who I genuinely enjoy and want to hang out with.
4. Likes animals, especially cats, in particular, my cat.
5. Likes going to beach, music, watching bands, playing tennis, going to the movies, seeing stand-up comedians, bushwalking, zoos, theme parks and exploring new things.
6. Can cook.
7. Enjoys a night in alone together drinking wine and playing board games just as much as

| | |
|---|---|
| | partying with friends.<br>8. Makes me laugh really hard every day.<br>9. Is entrepreneurial, adventurous, positive and enthusiastic.<br>10. Has a great smile, cute bum, and mischievous eyes – smiles at me and listens to me like I'm the only girl in the world for him.<br>11. Wears nice clothes.<br>12. Is a good driver.<br>13. Regularly compliments me.<br>14. Does half the house duties without me having to ask.<br>15. Is happy to financially support our family while we have children so I can be a full-time carer.<br>16. Likes trail bike riding and camping – and I feel safe being on the back of his bike.<br>17. Knows how to use a chainsaw and wants to live on acreage.<br>18. Is fun when they're drunk, and if they're not, acknowledge this and limit their alcohol intake. |
| **Self-Work** | 1. Finalise my settlement with Max.<br>2. Make some single friends and pursue my interests.<br>3. Lose weight and increase my fitness.<br>4. Learn better communication strategies.<br>5. Explore stress management and my compulsive need to help others at my expense. |
| **Meeting Potential Love Interests** | **Things I could do to increase my chances:**<br>1. Join local groups in my interests – music, guitar, social activism, bushwalking.<br>2. Start an invite-only Singles Group on Facebook.<br>3. Join Newcastle Singles Social Group. |

4. Prepare an online profile – refer to my Critical and Negotiable Personal Values when answering the questions.
5. Keep busy so I don't get lonely.
6. Relax about dating, have fun with it, don't take it too seriously. This is fun, not a chore, and I don't want to rush into a relationship with the wrong person and end up wasting my time.
7. While dating, practise open-ended questions to explore compatibility on Critical and Negotiable Personal Values.

| **Chunking down – the actions / how** | | **ACTIONS**<br>Target Due Date – set achievable timeframes<br><br>Date Completed |
|---|---|---|
| **1** | Finalise my settlement with Max. | 1. Phone Max and discuss what's holding up the settlement.<br>2. See if we can reach agreement.<br>3. If not, arrange an independent negotiator to sit with us both and finalise it.<br>4. Move quickly on all paperwork. |

| | | |
|---|---|---|
| **2** | Make some single friends and pursue my interests. | 1. Invite the three singles at work to start an invite-only Singles Group and keep things moving by immediately organising a fun social invite – perhaps a concert in the vineyards.<br>2. Visit the 3 music groups I've been interested in, and then choose one to join.<br>3. Join Newcastle Singles Social Group and attend at least one of their outings a month. |
| **3** | Lose weight and increase my fitness. | 1. Do the Michelle Bridges 12-week body challenge. Ask my friend Sonia to do it with me.<br>2. Join Newcastle Bushwalking and go on a walk at least once a month.<br>3. Re-join the local |

| | | |
|---|---|---|
| | | tennis and golf social comps and play weekly. |
| **4** | Learn better communication strategies. | 1. Join Toastmasters.<br>2. Read *The 5 Love Languages*, and *How to Win Friends and Influence People*.<br>3. Practise open-ended questions while dating.<br>4. Step back and take notice of my relationships and who puts as much effort into me as I put into them. |
| **5** | Explore stress management and my need to help others at my expense. | 1. Take advantage of the five free counselling sessions through work. Make the booking.<br>2. Evaluate after the free sessions if I need anything further.<br>3. Attend weekly yoga and actively |

| | | |
|---|---|---|
| | | learn more about the meditation component. |
| **6** | Meeting potential love interests. | In addition to the actions in point 2:<br><br>1. Put up an online profile with a current photo.<br>2. Never say no to any reasonable social invitation, even from couples – you just never know who I might meet while out. |

Keep a journal and refer back to this Action Plan weekly to track progress and adjust where necessary.

And lastly, some thoughts to leave you with …

# Releasing Your Past

I would like to introduce you to the power and complexities of your subconscious mind and an alternative therapy you might consider to assist in changing patterns of behaviour that are not working for you – hypnotherapy.

This is but a taste of a complex topic. The subconscious mind and its spectacular workings is a vast topic that is very interesting to explore further should you have the interest. I'm going to explain in a most basic way the surface of an intricate topic.

Have you ever been driving, and suddenly realised that you've arrived at your destination and you don't fully remember getting there? This feeling occurs because you're so experienced at driving, that your subconscious mind was able to look after that task for you, while your conscious mind was largely occupied thinking about whatever thoughts were uppermost in your mind. This is a form of hypnosis. You're not unconscious when hypnotised. Rather, you're tapped into your subconscious mind, but still aware of what is happening around you.

This can work both to your advantage and your disadvantage. Throughout our lives, especially when our emotions are aroused, our experiences implant lessons learned in our subconscious mind. At times, our subconscious mind operates automatically without our conscious mind being involved.

For instance, you may have had an emotionally charged moment as a child when you cleaned the house for your parents but you were unsure how they would react because you used the vacuum cleaner and you weren't actually allowed to use electrical appliances without one of them being present. When they came home and saw your efforts they were incredibly proud of you. Your nervousness vanished. A powerful lesson may have been implanted into your subconscious mind, and thereafter you became a person confident to take calculated risks to achieve good outcomes.

That is a positive outcome of hypnosis on the subconscious mind.

However, had your parents come home and chastised you, thereafter, you may have become a person who couldn't take any risks at all, and you've never been able to understand why you're like that, especially since you have friends and colleagues who repeatedly demonstrate to you how rewarding calculated risks can be.

A similar phenomenon can be occurring in your love relationships, particularly if you can see that you are repeatedly making the same mistakes. You know you keep doing it, but you're not sure why you behave in that way. To give you an example, if a girl's father ran off with another woman when she was a girl, her young mind may have interpreted this as being that *all* men are untrustworthy, and implanted this lesson in her subconscious mind. As a rational adult, her conscious mind knows that *all* men aren't untrustworthy, however, no matter who she's dating, she doesn't trust them when they go out without her, and it repeatedly causes problems in her relationships.

Hypnotherapy is a collaborative effort between you and a therapist which allows you to explore your subconscious mind to uncover lessons learned that may be hindering, rather than enhancing your life. Through hypnotherapy you may discover things about yourself that you previously didn't consciously recognise. Once you identify these automatic behaviours that are holding you back, hypnotherapy offers a vehicle through which you can change them.

Hypnotherapy is but one of a multitude of alternative therapies that might assist you in moving forward free of previous barriers.

The Australian Natural Therapists Association's website has a list of therapies that you might explore. Certainly, if something is holding you back, there is help available to you. There are also many excellent counsellors and psycologists who specialise in relationships, identity and behaviour. Explore what is around. Get recommendations from family and friends about what worked for them. Learning is a liberating thing, and letting go of emotional blockages is a truly empowering experience that will change your life.

You know yourself if you're in a place that you could benefit from additional support. If you are, seek it out. The results will liberate you.

## Tips for Combating Loneliness

The tips below are a compilation of the themes derived from the research interviews. Some of these have appeared throughout the Shared Stories. Some are new. This is an ideas bank to stimulate your own imagination.

1. Never say "no" to any reasonable invitation from friends, family or work colleagues. Each time you accept an invitation your network extends. When you decline invitations you miss opportunities for meeting new people and for experiencing those get-togethers that are surprisingly more enjoyable than anticipated.
2. Travel. Experienced travellers know that there is no other feeling like visiting somewhere new and different to your usual environment. Travel is soul food. Liberating. Rejuvenating. Empowering.
3. Join a local group for something you're interested in. The types of groups that are available to join are as vast as the number of interests. 4WDing, book appreciation, writing, sailing, betting, dance, sport, running, bushwalking, fishing, theatre, social groups for your age group, gem fossicking, travel, photography, singing, ukulele, art, motor bike riding, car restoration, cars … The list is endless. Most districts have active social community groups. If you try one and don't like it, don't be disheartened – try a different group. If you can't find what you're looking for in your region, start your own.
4. Volunteer for a cause you believe in. A female rural fire fighter described how empowered she felt learning how to use a fire hose and chainsaw, and driving the fire truck with lights and sirens on. She described the sense of camaraderie after spending hours upon hours fighting a bushfire and 'having each other's back' out in the field. She didn't find a love interest at her brigade, but her newfound confidence attracted her next partner when she met him.
5. Enrol in a short course and physically attend the classes. You'll not meet anyone doing an online course.
6. For working professionals, join a business networking group.

Caroline from Chapter 8 made a large network of friends in a new town simply by doing this.

7. Be good company. Listen as much as you talk. Show interest in others around you. You'll get more invitations if you do this, than if you constantly regale everyone around you about your ex and your pain. It's okay to talk about yourself and your own experiences, just be sure you return the favour and show genuine interest in the life of the person who just listened to you.
8. Enrol to do a motivational course. Have you ever talked to anyone who has been to an Anthony Robbins seminar for instance? Their energy is contagious.
9. Hire a sports car and go on a weekend road trip; perhaps with a mate or family member who's good company. Let the top down.
10. If you're a lady wanting to meet men, think about where men congregate; eg. 4WD clubs, tennis, golf, football and soccer members stands, beer festivals, SES, Rural Fire Brigade, bowls, ten pin bowling. If you're a man wanting to meet women think dance, cooking, tennis, book clubs, fashion parades, concerts, bowls, yoga retreats, etc.
11. Get yourself a wingman/woman. Choose carefully, remembering that if you take them out with you, they are a reflection to others of the type of people you surround yourself with.
12. Set yourself fitness targets, and push yourself to meet them. Not only will you feel your best, you'll look your best too.
13. Don't let a tight budget stop you from getting out there. Remember back to your teenage years – you had little money but a bucket full of fun. It costs next to nothing to take up jogging and join a local running group. It costs nothing to volunteer at the local zoo, to take up cycling and join a group, invite your friends to free city events. Be proactive. Your next love is not going to knock on your front door while you're at home eating chocolate and pizza or drinking beer and watching the football. Now is your chance to design the life you want; to involve yourself with people with similar interests to yours. Google local social groups, opportunities and events.
14. Be inventive, do something similar to Stacey like starting your own closed Facebook singles group.

15. Resist, resist, resist the urge to be 'desperate' to meet a partner. Revel in each new experience and wonderful personality that you meet, whether they turn out to be a new platonic friend or a possible love interest. Love *will* happen. No matter your age or circumstances, there are others out there in a similar position to yourself. 30 – 90+, with a sparkle in your step, and a glint in your eye, there are always other singles to meet. And no matter how things might seem right now, if you do at least some of the steps above, you just never know what exciting adventure is just around the corner for you.

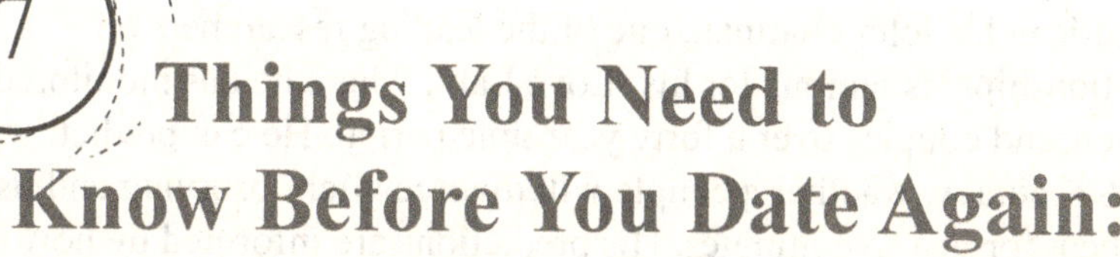

# 7 Things You Need to Know Before You Date Again:

1. Choosing your next partner is a decision that could potentially impact your life for years to come. It's an important decision that deserves due attention.
2. Aligned Personal Values are essential for an enduring love relationship.
3. We all have two types of Personal Values: Critical (Non-Negotiable) and Negotiable.
4. In order to know if another's Personal Values are aligned to yours, you must first know what your own Critical and Negotiable Personal Values are.
5. Entering a new relationship simply because you're lonely will likely take you on a path you later regret.
6. Positive versus negative communication should ideally be 80:20 respectively for happy, enduring relationships. Open-ended questions are a good strategy to practise.
7. With a few more smarts under your belt now, Happiness is yours to grasp.

# Recommended Resource

American Dr John Gottman, one of the leading researchers on relationships, is famous for his 'Love Lab', where he has monitored over a thousand couples over a forty year time period. He can predict, with 91% accuracy, whether a couple will divorce after observing and listening to them for just five minutes. His predictions are informed by how the couple communicate and interact with each other. He advises that couples need a ratio of 80:20 of positive versus negative communication. He's developed a model called 'The Sound Relationship House'. I recommend his book and DVD 'Making Relationships Work' for further reading and viewing.

If you engaged with this book, please consider submitting a review on Amazon. We'd love to hear your thoughts.

*Finding Love Again* is available for purchase from www.hawkeyepublishing.com.au

Join *Finding Love Again* on Facebook or follow the *Finding Love Again* Blog.

# Acknowledgements

I wish to acknowledge and thank all the people who kindly agreed to be interviewed for this book. Whilst they can't be named to protect the identities of speakers and others they've mentioned in their Shared Stories, they know who they are, and they've contributed to a book that will hopefully help others navigate what can be a challenging time in life, but one full of possibilities. From me to you - thank you!

Writing books is not easy. This book took three years to research and write, and I couldn't have done it without the support network of people around me. In particular, I wish to thank my husband Saul Martinez, and my friend, Michael Neilson, for their unwavering belief in me, and ongoing encouragement. Michael's unwavering support and encouragement of me in work-based situations has enhanced my confidence to achieve things once thought impossible. My husband's strong belief in this book and my writing kept me going at times when it all seemed too much.

I also wish to thank those who volunteered their time to add their own unique talents to *Finding Love Again*. Particularly the very talented photographer Stewart Hazell who spent days taking and processing photographs. Thank you to all the models and beta readers mentioned at the beginning of *Finding Love Again*, and also to those who agreed to have their photo taken but don't appear in the book. To the many friends and colleagues who shared my advertisements for interviewees and volunteers via social media - you guys rock.

I feel incredibly grateful for all your efforts in helping to bring *Finding Love* to fruition.

# About the Author

Carolyn Martinez is an Author and former Newspaper Editor who has had a break-up and re-found love. Due to the profound effect these experiences had on her life, and the number of people around her struggling with similar, she researched *Finding Love Again* and compiled a book of experiences with robust examples. The suggestions contained in this book are valuable and consistent with current thinking.

Carolyn's first book, *Inspiring IVF Stories*, was published in 2011. She has a Master of Arts (Writing) through Swinburne University, Victoria, Australia.

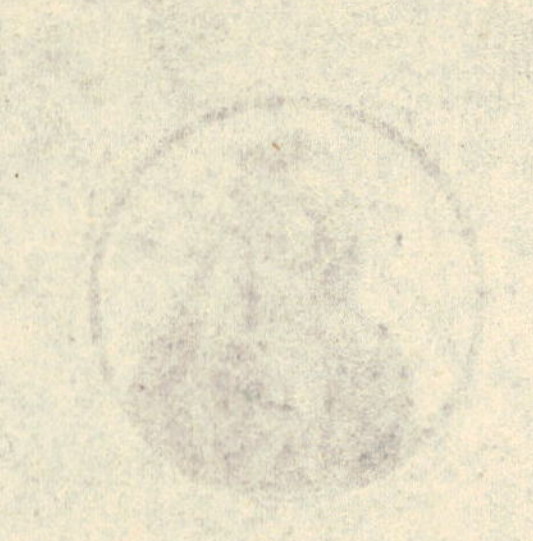